With *SAW, PLANE & CHISEL*

How to Build HISTORIC AMERICAN FURNITURE *With Hand Tools*

ZACHARY DILLINGER

POPULAR WOODWORKING BOOKS

CINCINNATI, OHIO

popularwoodworking.com

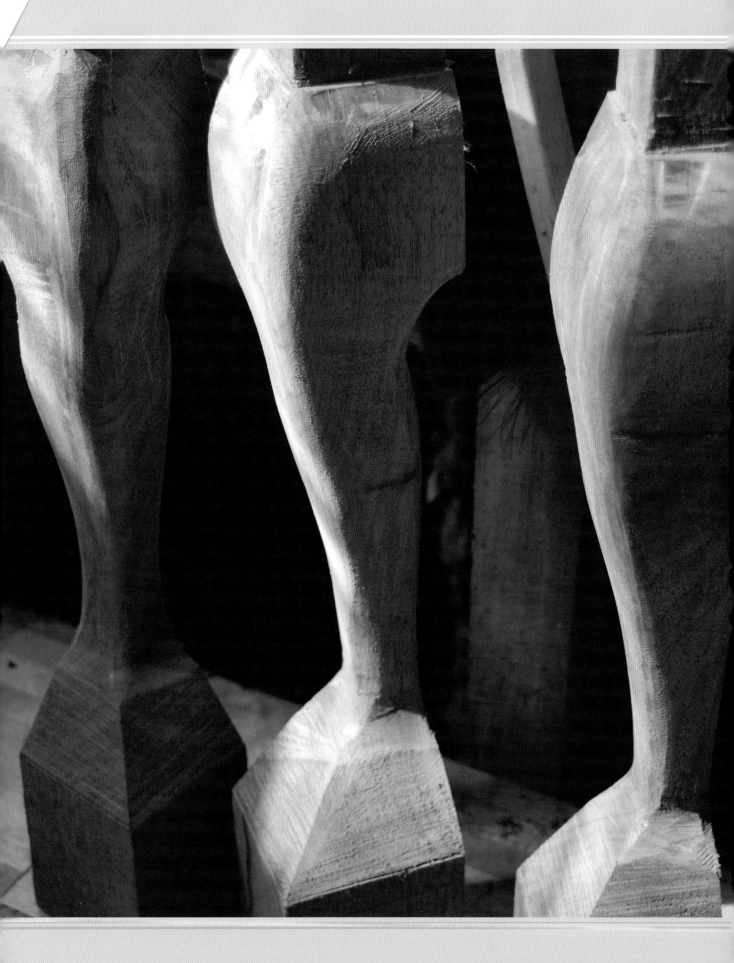

With SAW, PLANE & CHISEL

How to Build HISTORIC AMERICAN FURNITURE
With Hand Tools

ZACHARY DILLINGER

CONTENTS

THOUGHTS ON CRAFT

Hardware
by Nancy Cogger

Period Furniture Styles:
A Historian's Perspective
by Robert F. Trent

FOREWORD

We were so clever back in the 1960s.
In a Nixon-era book on fixing up old furniture, I once read:
"Your old woodworker was a mighty clever fellow! When he built a chair, he would always choose a glue that was weaker than the wood. That way, when the chair broke, it was the glue that gave way, but the joint remained intact. All he had to do was glue it back!"

So here's the picture that statement paints: It's the year 1780 and "Your old woodworker" stands at his bench ready to glue his chair together. He must choose carefully! He reaches for the clear bottle of Ye Glue Super – but stays his hand. "Nay. T'would be too strong," he mutters. His fingers move towards the jar of Old Yeller Tightly Bonding, but again he hesitates. "Nay. I must build weakness into my chair!" He glances at the twin tubes of A Pox of E! and shakes his head in wonderment at the bounteous choices available to him here in 1780! He knows what he must do, and as one hand dabs his brush into the old iron pot of hide glue weakened by the addition of old cheese and stale beer, his other hand strains to reach around and pat himself on his back.

To top this scene off, the photo of the broken chair seat accompanying the text showed a cheap, factory-made butt joint spanned by a pair of glue-globbed, spiral-cut dowels. The nearest "your old woodworker" probably got to this particular chair was cursing it as it broke under his weight at the old folks home.

This is the curse of presentism, the projection of our own cleverness onto the past, and we cannot escape it. The past is truly a foreign country that we can never visit, but as with the old maps decorated with fanciful creatures populating unknown lands, we fill in the unknowable past with needs from our own time. Yes, we always try to do better, to find a more accurate representation of the past, but our best efforts always seem to reveal less about the past than about our present selves.

That is why "With Saw, Plane & Chisel" brings such good news about the times we live in today. This is not a book you would have seen in the 1960s, that distant age of motorized fishing lures, the music of J. S. Bach played on synthesizers, and high-speed, rotary, combustion-powered ways to do everything. But that was how we got to now. The technology of the jet age brought us to this point of "peak stuff." Now the experience of our bodies at work has become a welcome joy. Between our hand and the wood, we now can seek that old connection, finding the most elegant and elemental instruments to carry our conversation with nature – the saw, the plane and the chisel. Our dialogue of building is once again free-flowing, but not without direction. Every stroke of the plane informs the next one. Each cut adjusts to fit the one made before it. Every piece of work that you complete shows that your mind and body was there at every moment of the creation.

This book will keep you in good company as you work. There are fine pieces for you to build, spanning the great ages of American woodworking. These projects may surprise you if you are expecting baby-steps, for Zach takes you from proper hand tool technique right into building the most excellent pieces. But have courage, traveller! Because Zach confidently speaks the old language of hand tools and wood, he will show you a safe and true path to follow as you meet each worthy challenge on this fine journey.

It's been a winding road that led us here. Back in the sixties, there was a home power tool that boasted "The Skill is in the Machine!" So, I guess they thought we not only wanted a pitching machine for batting practice, but a hitting machine as well so we could just sit back and watch. But the desire for skill has never left us, and the effort required to achieve it still earns the greatest respect. We no more expect to just pick up a chisel and do perfect work than we expect to pick up a recorder and play Bach the first time out. The work is ours to enjoy.

Zach brings us woodworking as great music, now played again on the original instruments. This art is indeed of a specific time, but it somehow stands outside of time as well. The timeless reward resides not just in the product, but also in the process. We listen again to the sound of the saw, and once again, the sound of our work delights our hearing rather than damaging it. We can hear in our work the sharpness of the edge, the grain and seasoning of the wood. The wood and the tools speak to us as we work. Sometimes I fancy that they ask "Hey! Where have you been? There's work to be done!"

Don't worry fellas! We're back!

—*Roy Underhill*

Why & How To Build Period Furniture

I work with period furniture because of the stories these pieces tell. From the simplest nailed blanket chest to the most elaborate Chippendale secretary, each surviving piece is a physical manifestation of a turbulent, dangerous, yet vibrant era in our history — among the only tangible objects that remain, in fact. With a little knowledge and skill, you can also learn to trace the hand of the maker in these pieces. Machine tools didn't dictate the composition or execution. The furniture looks handmade because it is handmade.

In order to successfully understand, appreciate and ultimately reproduce the pieces we will study, it is imperative to understand both the construction and the domestic context of the originals. They were built by professional and semi-professional artisans for whom making furniture was a means of survival, not an enjoyable hobby. They worked long hours in less than ideal settings, often in poor light, to produce salable goods. Attention could not be lavished on every surface, and every joint was not flawless (the idea of a "piston-fit" drawer didn't arrive until the studio furniture movement of the mid-20th century). In short, these men and women were making a living producing the best work they could within considerable limitations.

Being consumer goods, these pieces had to meet the demands of the customer. That reality connects them closely to their time period, if you know what to look for. The fact that period houses lacked electric lighting and climate control explains many of the construction techniques and imperfections. The carved, inlaid and veneered ornamentation speak of a society that valued conspicuous consumption. Perhaps even more interesting are the pieces that can only aspire to that status, simulating expensive decorative techniques with the skillful use of paint — and relying on a fair bit of eye-squint in the candlelit rooms of the time. These pieces speak of a middle class that envied the latest fashions of the well-heeled, letting us look back 200 years to glimpse a society that shared many of our own motivations.

Perfect imperfection

Eighteenth-century furniture, even the most celebrated pieces in the finest museums, exhibits a significant amount of "flaws," at least by the modern definition. The simple fact is that the period reproductions we make today can be executed better than the pieces produced by our ancestors. But what constitutes a "flaw," or a "better" level of execution, depends on who is looking.

Falling below today's standard of acceptability, period surfaces show handplane tear-out without obvious attempts to scrape or plane it away. Boards often are not flat and have non-parallel faces and edges. That's because they didn't need to work with the straight fences and precision-ground work surfaces of modern machines. On interior surfaces the story of the saw pit is often left untouched. Boards cup, sometimes enough to tear off hinges, because the original builder didn't account sufficiently for seasonal wood movement, not to mention the invention of central climate-control. And drawer runners were often nailed onto case sides across the grain because that simply took less time than making a dadoed runner.

While the surviving work of the past may have cracked or split, the fact that these pieces still exist more than 200 years later makes them true success stories, no matter how "flawed" their construction seems to modern critics.

Since my goal is to make pieces that look as much like the originals as possible, I don't concern myself with the modern definition of a "flaw." My final surfaces sometimes show that same minor amount of tear-out. My mouldings are not identical from one linear foot to the next, and they sometimes warp a little. My boards aren't perfectly flat when they don't have to be. They are efficiently worked just enough to do what I need them to do, and therein, to fully record the tools and labor that made the piece possible. No more, no less.

By the way, this approach is also what makes working by hand as fast or faster than using power tools. Many modern woodworkers seek the extremely high levels of perfection made possible with modern tools, but then express frustration with how slow hand tool methods are by comparison. I readily admit they are slow when using them to achieve that kind of perfection, but this is an inappropriate use of the technology.

The key to your success and satisfaction is calibrating your mind to pre-power tool ways. Period artisans did not have the luxury of chasing perfection. They were paid to produce furniture, not infinitesimally thin plane shavings or the world's most perfect dovetailed drawer. Therefore, perfection for perfection's sake is, in fact, imperfect when it comes to accurately reproducing period furniture. It is easy to focus solely on the details along the way, and to allow the pursuit of perfection to obscure the goal of creating a unified piece. In the end, you produce an also-ran.

Why hand tools?

To achieve the imperfect perfection of realistic period work, I use only hand tools. In my opinion, replicating 18th-century pieces means doing the work only with tools that were available to artisans of the period, namely wooden hand planes, Western-style saws and chisels with period-correct attributes (i.e. tanged handles and square sides).

I'm certainly not judging power tools or modern versions of period tools as improper in every case; they just don't fit with my goal of maintaining period accu-racy. Call me a hardcore purist, a Galoot, a Luddite, whatever you choose. Ultimately, your tooling decision is just that, yours.

For me, power tools leave a piece looking more modern and less like the work of the past. It is more than just the quality of the surfaces. While you can handplane or sand away planer marks and table saw cuts to give a "period correct" surface, designing and building with only hand tools, when properly done, yields a piece that looks handmade because of the overall integration of imperfection into a pleasing final form. Achieving this goal is extraordinarily difficult when using fenced and jigged power tools. Machines make boards, joints and mouldings that stand out as too perfect on period pieces.

The freedom of the hand-tool approach permeates the process, starting at the outset. Design decisions can be based on the existing material specifications rather than a nominal dimension on a plan. You don't have to design a piece to exact dimensions; you can make it work with the wood you have on hand. You don't expend your limited energy and time to plane a $7/8$"-thick board down to $3/4$" just because this is the dimension you see in the plan. You make $7/8$" work.

This is not a condemnation of power tools; they simply don't fit with my goals for reproducing antiques. If you have different goals, please adapt the construction chapters as necessary to use the tooling you prefer. The fundamental information on using hand tools to make furniture is equally applicable to those woodworkers who take a hybrid approach. But for me, the limitations of hand tools are more than offset by the sheer enjoyment of their use, and the human quality of the work they produce.

Please note that this book is not intended to teach you how to restore, sharpen or tune hand tools. There are many sources available already, some of which I will point you to, that do a fine job of addressing these topics. In these pages, you will not learn how to make a handsaw cut properly or how to sharpen a chisel effectively. Instead, you will be reading my methods

for using sharp and true hand tools to make equally sharp and true furniture.

These six pieces are just a start

There are many fine books on the topic of period furniture reproduction. You will find a large list of my favorites in the final chapter. However, many of these works introduce modern aesthetic choices and methods, and, most troubling to the period purist, often change period designs to suit the needs of modern tools.

I've written "With Saw, Plane & Chisel" to add a new voice to the conversation, creating a jumping-off point for historically-accurate furniture reproduction.

While I can't pretend to have provided an exhaustive account of this historic craft, I have attempted to faithfully and accurately demonstrate the techniques I used to make six furniture projects – techniques that can be used to replicate almost any piece of furniture you like. You will also learn enough to incorporate authentic elements of period work into your own designs.

I'll give the history of each of the 18th-century styles I present, as well as advice on period-correct tools, methods for how to prepare stock and cut solid

joinery and details of authentic ornamentation techniques. My goal is to make the craft accessible to everyone, to clarify the confusing and to contemporize the historic, so that you can begin to enjoy this worthy pursuit as much as I do.

I hope that you will take the information and techniques I provide here, challenge yourself to seek out and experiment with different techniques and ideas, and ultimately come up with your own way of working. As with many things in life, in woodworking there is no one right way to do anything. In my opinion, there is also no wrong way to do anything as long you achieve your goals without compromising your intent. If you fail, try again. If you succeed completely and easily, ask if you challenged yourself enough.

Although you will find measured drawings and cut lists for all six pieces, please think about working out the necessary dimensions for yourself from just the pictures and major dimensions. While this is not an easy task, it will increase your ability to understand how the period furniture process works.

The bottom line is this: I'm asking you to question your own definition of the word craftsmanship and to expand your skill set. This is not a call to do poor work, something which was no more acceptable in the period than it is today. Instead, I challenge you to try for something more esoteric than "perfect" dovetails and "piston fit" drawers: something true.

Finally, my goal for this book is to provide you with a better understanding of how and, perhaps more importantly, why things were done, and expand your interest in period furniture. I hope you will study the pieces of the past and see them for what they are: snapshots of a moment in time, which can teach us about the men and women who lived and worked in this country more than 200 years ago.

It is my sincere hope that this book will provide you with enough information to get you started on the right foot, and, as an 18th-century candlestand maker would have said, "put your best foot forward."

The rest of the journey is up to you.

TECHNIQUES

CHAPTER ONE

Preparing Stock by Hand

The hand-tool woodworker is faced with a daunting challenge from the start: Preparing wood by hand is time-consuming, physically challenging work. And without properly prepared materials, any furniture project is doomed to fail.

The solution is simple: Do only as much as necessary. Eighteenth-century artisans knew this, as evidenced by the varying levels of stock preparation on period pieces. Some surfaces are planed smooth and flat; others show rough saw marks or heavy plane tracks and tear-out.

The most important lesson to learn about efficient hand tool usage is that not every surface is prominent (called a "show" surface) in the finished piece.

Therefore, some faces can be left rough, others can be planed only minimally, while others should be as flat and smooth as possible. By the way, I generally work with rough-sawn lumber, as did period makers of the past.

To make it clear exactly how much to work various surfaces, I've come up with a classification system that I will use throughout the rest of the book. Of course, you are free to process the boards to a higher level if you so desire. As you grow in experience, you will instinctually know how much to work each surface and won't need to refer to this system anymore. But I hope you'll try it out for a while.

My surface classification system is as follows:

The underside of this c.1770 tea table shows uniform plane marks from a finely set smoothing plane. These marks are amplified in raking light.

The underside of the interior floor of the c.1770 Pennsylvania desk shows heavy plane marks and significant tear-out.

Heavy plane tracks and the telltale sign of a nicked plane iron appear on the backboard of this c.1800 dressing table.

Tear-out on a show surface? This c.1770 Pennsylvania desk lid has it in spades.

This desk bottom board has horrible tear-out and plane tracks, and the piece has some of the poorest dovetails I've ever seen. Yet it survives more than 200 years later.

Class I: Smooth, square, flat, usually parallel to the opposing surface with little to no tool marks or tear-out. This is reserved for your most prominent show surfaces where substantial thickness variation, tool marks or plane tear-out would be especially noticeable.

Class II: A smooth, somewhat flat surface with nothing more than light tool marks left by the passage of the plane. The surface may not be perfectly flat or straight but appears to be so with the naked eye. In period work most show surfaces have Class II characteristics.

Class III: A straight, flat, square surface or edge with light tool marks or tear-out, not necessarily parallel to its opposing face or edge.

Class IV: An overall flat and straight surface with moderate to heavy tool marks.

Class V: The raw, unprocessed surface of the board. The surface exhibits sawmill marks or tear-out from the riving process.

A Class I surface, showing a perfectly smooth surface. No tearout, no plane marks, just gleaming wood.

The Class II surface appears to be flat and shows just a bit of plane tracks. This level of surface preparation is correct for most period show surfaces.

A Class III surface. This is the perfect reference surface.

There are heavy tool marks and plane tracks on this Class IV board. It is good enough for non-show surfaces such as a case interior or a bottom board.

It is bad form to leave this Class V surface on a piece of furniture, but only because the circular saw marks are out of place on 18th-century furniture. Plane them off immediately!

The measuring tools of the craft. Top row, from left: striking (marking) knife, large dividers, small dividers, mortising gauge, marking gauge and folding rule. Front row, from left: winding sticks, small shop-made square, large shop-made square, shop-made bevel gauge, and two dovetail marking tools (square and angle gauge).

Essential hand saws, from top: crosscut saw filed with 8 teeth per inch, a ripsaw with 5½ teeth per inch, a crosscut saw with 10 teeth per inch, and a large ripsaw with 5 teeth per inch. These are the workhorses of a hand-tool shop.

A 19th-century-style handle on a Lakeside ripsaw. This handle shape is comfortable enough to use for extended periods of time.

Another important component, one that goes hand in hand with minimizing surface preparation and working quickly by hand, is recognizing how accurately you need to size pieces. If you are trying to reproduce an existing piece of furniture exactly, obviously the overall size of the parts will be dictated by the original. However, if you are designing your own work, whether period-inspired or not, you can design and build it to suit the lumber you have available, and accept any deviations that crop up along the way. It often doesn't matter exactly how thick a board is since each board in a project is cut to fit its mate or neighbor as the project progresses.

Essential tools for stock prep

The process begins with measuring and marking, using tools like those shown in **Photo 1**. You will need mark-ing gauges, a folding rule, a pair of winding sticks, a few accurate squares and a straightedge. These tools are all available new, or you can make them in your shop. To get started making furniture as quickly as possible, I recommend that you buy these tools. Tool-making can evolve into a completely different hobby if you aren't careful!

For cutting stock to size, you will need at least two saws: a ripsaw and a crosscut saw (**Photo 2**). The crosscut saw is for cutting your stock to rough length. Some woodworkers like a panel-sized saw, meaning between 20" and 24" long, while others prefer a full-size, 26" saw. I prefer the full-size saw for crosscutting stock to rough length, but for more precise cuts at the bench (more on that in the Joinery chapter) I turn to panel saws or even backsaws.

I recommend that the ripsaw be around 26" in length with 5½ to 8 teeth per inch. This will work for all ripping duties featured in this book. Don't get too worked up about the specifications of the saw; spend more time finding a saw with a comfortable grip that won't give you blisters. See **Photo 3** for an idea of what to look for in a saw handle.

For flattening and smoothing stock, you will need a set of bench planes, including a fore plane for the initial planing, a try plane for ensuring flatness and straightness of faces and edges, and a smooth plane for the final touches on Class I and Class II surfaces (**see Photos 4-7**). These are all the planes you need to prepare stock effectively, but it certainly doesn't hurt to have more.

You will also need a solid woodworking bench to hold the work while you are planing it and cutting joints (**Photo 8**). Several excellent books have been written about workbenches, and I will not attempt to rewrite them here. I recommend that you pick up Chris

4

5

Smoothing planes, from left: a 19th-century American 45° smoothing plane, a modern American 55° smoothing plane, a small 50° English smoothing plane from the early 20th century, and a 19th-century Dutch-style "gerfschaaf" plane.

A full bench-plane lineup, from left: a group of smoothing planes, three jointer and try planes, and a group of fore and jack planes.

6

Fore and jack planes, from left: a shop-made Dutch-style "voor-looper" set to take a medium-fine shaving, a smaller "roffelschaaf" set to take coarse shavings, and a 19th-century British jack plane set to take very coarse shavings.

7

The long bench planes, from front: a 19th-century British try plane, an 18th-century English jointer plane, and a shop-made 30" jointer plane in the early American style.

The center of my shop universe, an 8'-long Roubo/Nicholson hybrid bench. It has a thick top that withstands anything I can throw at it, along with a tall apron to support boards on edge. This bench is a wonderful partner and I couldn't work without it.

Schwarz's "Workbenches: From Design & Theory to Construction & Use." My bench is a hybrid of two of the benches discussed in that book: It has a Roubo-style top with a Nicholson-type apron. It works very well for my needs as a period furniture-maker.

Finally, without a doubt, your most important tools are your brain and body. With a little experience, your hands will be sensitive enough to feel when a surface isn't flat (**Photo 9**). Your eyes are sharp enough to detect minute variations from square or to see twist across a pair of winding sticks. Finally, your brain will let you know when you can stop working a surface, and help you grasp the concept of reference edges.

Focus your attention on two surfaces, not four

When preparing lumber by hand, it is very time-consuming to achieve opposite faces that are absolutely flat and parallel to each other at some exact thickness. Things will go much faster if you become familiar with the concept of reference surfaces. A reference surface is simply a face or edge (you'll need one of each) that you focus your time and effort on, taking it to a Class III preparation.

You need to rely on those surfaces being flat, straight and square to each other. For one thing, they might be the only surfaces that show, and thus the only ones that really matter. And for another, those surfaces are the ones you'll be taking all measurements from, and using to lay out all cuts and joinery. The success of your project depends on your ability to make and use these reference surfaces correctly. That's why you should always mark those edges with a pencil once they are completed, for easy identification later (**Photo 10**).

With a little training, you can learn to feel high spots in a board. Fingertips are among the most useful measuring tools in a period furniture shop.

10

A sample board with the markings I use on a daily basis. I don't usually label them; a simple mark on each surface is sufficient.

11

I often use sidewalk chalk to mark out rough crosscuts when breaking down stock to size. It holds up better than a pencil, and works well when precision isn't necessary.

Prepping parts is just a series of steps

I typically buy my lumber in 8' lengths and as wide as possible. These boards can be difficult to store and unwieldy to move, so I reduce the boards to the necessary rough sizes as soon as I get them back to my shop. Since things can change once a project gets underway, you shouldn't cut all of your parts to the exact sizes on a stock list. Instead, to give yourself flexibility later, include some extra length and width when sawing the pieces to rough size. In general, I add about 1" to the length and 1" to the width.

Saw each part to rough size

To begin, measure the board using the folding rule and square and make layout lines with the marking knife, chalk or pencil if you prefer (**Photo 11**). Never saw a board without first laying out the line you want to cut, and always saw to the waste side of that line. This applies to all hand sawing, though it is most important when cutting joinery. By practicing it now, while rough-sawing, you will learn to saw to a line when it matters most.

My technique for rough-sawing, whether ripping or crosscutting, relies on keeping my head and most importantly my left eye (I saw left-handed; if you saw right-handed, use your right eye) directly over the cut as much as possible. To enable this orientation, I use a low saw bench to hold the lumber.

To be sure you are starting the saw square to the board, use your try square as shown in **Photo 12**, and periodically check your saw against the square as you proceed. Make full strokes, using as much of the saw as possible.

For crosscuts, I keep the saw angled about 45° from vertical (**Photo 13**); and for rip cuts I use a more

12

When starting a saw cut, in this case a crosscut, use your try square to orient the blade. Until you develop the muscle and eye memory to make square cuts, check the saw for square periodically when cutting.

13

When crosscutting, I like to keep the saw at about 45° from vertical. This helps me keep the blade on the line and is aggressive enough to make quick work of the cut.

14

Ripsawing calls for a more aggressive angle of attack, in this case about 20° from vertical.

15

To correct an errant saw cut, bring the saw down to 70° from vertical. This puts more of the saw plate in the cut and helps bring it back in line.

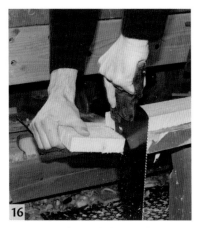

16

Using your off-hand, hold the offcut in place to prevent splintering the wood when the saw exits the cut.

17

Here I am using a try plane, diagonally across the grain, to clean up the rough-sawn surface of a board. This reveals the high spots and also helps me determine which way the grain is running.

aggressive angle, about 20° from vertical (**Photo 14**). Should the saw drift off the line, drop this angle to 70° or so from vertical; this will let you use more of the length of the saw to direct the cut back to the line (**Photo 15**). Worry more about cutting to the line than about the speed of your progress. As you gain experience, your speed, accuracy and confidence will improve. When finishing the cut, make sure to support the waste piece with your off-hand or you will splinter out the bottom corner with the final push (**Photo 16**).

Flatten one face

Once a piece is cut to rough size on the saw bench, I move it to the workbench and choose a reference face. This depends a lot on the final use of the board, but in general, I put the prettiest face on the outside, That means knots and very tricky grain go on the inside face, which ends up being the reference face in most cases. So it needs to be flat and straight, but it can have tear-out and other cosmetic issues.

The reference face is where stock preparation begins. Since we are dealing with rough-sawn lumber, it is prudent to begin flattening that reference face by planing across the grain using a fore or try plane set for a medium shaving (**Photo 17**). This accomplishes two things: It gives you an idea of how flat the board is from the start, and it helps you to understand the grain better.

Grain tends to slope either upward or downward along the length of a board, and planing with the wood fibers instead of against them – like petting a cat front to back – will greatly reduce or eliminate tear-out. This

On this sample board, the grain changes directions at the large knot, causing significant tear-out.

18

19

Using my winding stick as a straightedge, I run it over the face of the board to find the high spots, marking them with a pencil (or chalk on a dark wood).

20

I use my fingertips to confirm the high spots I marked in pencil.

initial planing will help you figure out which way the grain is "running" (**see Photo 18**). It will also help you identify any curly grain or other figure in the wood that you may wish to accentuate in the project.

Once you have quickly planed the face, get your straightedge and run it over the surface to identify the high spots. I like to hold the straightedge on each end using my thumbs and forefingers and place it at the far end of the board. I then attempt to gently rock the straightedge side to side (**Photo 19**). If it rocks easily, it means that the edge is resting on a high spot. I mark this area with a pencil and then move the straightedge about an inch down the board at a time (**Photo 20**), repeating the rocking process until I have covered the

Using winding sticks to find twist requires kneeling down and sighting across the top of them.

21

The sticks show no twist in this board.

22

23

This picture shows a board that has a significant twist, with the high spot on the right.

24

This shows a board with an equal yet opposite twist, the high area being on the left.

25

Planing out the high spots I marked earlier.

26

The finished reference face.

entire length. I then use the fore plane again, cross-grain, to remove the high spots I marked. I then repeat the rock-and-move process again to ensure that the planing did its job. I also rock the straightedge at an angle to the grain; this helps me get the board flat along the grain as well, speeding my efforts in the next step.

The cross-grain planing ensures that the board is flat across its width but it does little to ensure that this first face is flat along its length. So I next reach for my winding sticks (see **Photos 21-24**) , which accentuate any twist. Put one stick on each end, and then sight along the top edges. If the board has twist, the tops of your sticks won't be parallel. Mark any high spots with a pencil, and then move the rear stick progressively closer to the front stick, sighting across both and marking any more high spots. I typically do this every 6" or so on a Class III reference surface; other classes may only require a couple of measurements.

With the twist identified, take your try plane, set for a medium cut, and plane down the grain, focusing your efforts on the high spots at first (**Photos 25, 26**) When planing along the length of a board, your hand pressure is important. At the start of the cut, you should place more pressure on the toe of the plane than the tote (the big handle in the back), in the middle of the cut you should have approximately equal hand pressure, and at the finish you should have more pressure on the tote (**Photos 27-29**). This will help you keep the plane level and in contact with the flattened surface throughout the stroke, preventing you from producing a rounded surface.

This is a good time to give the face one more check with the winding sticks. Once it looks good, and I can take full-length and full-width shavings down the length of the board, it is flat enough to use as my reference surface (**Photo 30**). I mark the surface as such and then identify which edge will serve as the reference edge.

To start a plane stroke, push down on the toe of the plane with 80% of your total hand pressure. This will help to keep the plane level.

In the middle of the cut, apply equal pressure with each hand. Also note that I am using my fingers as a fence to help me keep the plane and the edge square to the face.

To finish the stroke, let up pressure with your front hand, concentrating 80 percent of the pressure on your rear hand.

30

Full-length, full-width plane shavings show that the surface is as flat as possible, at least with the plane at hand. A finer-set plane might create a flatter surface, but efficiency and the board's ultimate use determine how flat it needs to be.

Joint one edge

When choosing my reference edge, I consider a couple of things. I think about how I want the grain on the show face to be oriented in the final piece of furniture, and I also look for the edge with the straightest grain, so I can plane it easily.

Place the board in your front vise, with the freshly planed reference face facing you. Place your try square against that reference face and check the reference edge in several places, including at each end and at several spots along the length of the board. It's unlikely that your edge will be square at any of those points but sometimes you get lucky and it is close. Next, use your winding sticks as you did before, sighting down them at various points along the edge's length to determine if it is twisted, and marking the obvious high spots with a pencil (**Photo 31**).

Now pick up your try plane again, set it for a light cut, and make a test pass down the edge. As described above, controlling your hand pressure is vital to achieving a flat surface. This is particularly true when jointing,

31

Use winding sticks to check the reference edge for twist. Closing one eye, as when shooting a gun, can sometimes help you see better. Funny faces are optional.

32

A full-length shaving shows that this edge is flat. The try square and winding sticks determine if it is square to the reference face.

which means to flatten and square an edge along its length. Take a couple of passes, and then check with the try square in several locations. Focus your efforts on the problem areas until the edge is square with the face in every test location. Finally, take one last full length shaving with the plane. This will ensure that the edge is square and straight down its length. This is now your reference edge (**Photo 32**).

Work the opposite faces for final sizing

You now have a board with one flat face and one straight edge square to that face. Using those reference surfaces, you can now bring the board to its final size. To size the board to the required width, use a marking gauge or its big brother, the panel gauge, to mark the opposing edge. Run the fence of the gauge against your reference edge and scribe your line. Then saw and plane to that line. This will be necessary for almost every board you process for furniture (**Photos 33-35**).

With power tools, it is very easy to run the board through a planer to achieve accurate thickness, without breaking a sweat. When working by hand, however, you have to ask yourself how important it is to achieve some nominal thickness for each board in a project. It isn't always necessary to thickness your board to a fixed dimension or even to flatten the opposite side of the workpiece at all. That said, the opposite face requires some level of processing on most boards.

33

Mark the width of the board next, using the reference edge as the bearing surface for the marking gauge.

34

Saw and/or plane the board to the marked line. I sometimes darken the marking gauge lines with a pencil.

35

Square and straighten this edge with the try plane.

Given that it often doesn't matter exactly how thick a board is (you can cut your joinery to match the thickness), you can often get away with simply planing the board to its greatest common dimension. To do this, set a marking gauge to the thinnest point of the board, place its fence against the reference face, and run it around all four edges (**Photo 36**).

Plane down close to the line with the fore plane for a Class IV surface (**Photo 37**). A board intended to be ¾" thick might end up ¹⁄₁₆" under or ⅛" over, if you even bother to measure, but this will usually have no effect on the overall success of the piece and you will have saved a lot of effort by not seeking machine-like precision with your handplanes.

Sometimes, however, a somewhat consistent thickness is important for aesthetics, and occasionally a board must be thicknessed to a specific dimension. To achieve this, just set your marking gauge to the desired dimension, and rough-plane it close to that line with the fore plane. If the face opposite the reference face is going to be the show face, work your way to a Class II or perhaps even a Class I surface using the try plane and smooth plane, working right up to the line. Use the try plane to knock down the obvious high spots, and then smooth any tear-out or plane tracks with the smooth plane, scrapers or sandpaper.

Now you have prepared a board just as a period craftsman would have done, and it is ready for joinery.

36

Scribe the greatest possible thickness of the board, using the reference face as the bearing surface for the marking gauge.

37

Rough-plane the board down to the scribed line. Depending on the use of the board, I may leave the Class IV surface or work it with the try and smooth planes to achieve a higher surface quality.

CHAPTER TWO

Period-correct Joinery

In the 18th century, when expediency was far more important than objective perfection, things were done that wouldn't pass muster today. However, given my goal of authentic reproduction, I follow the same so-called "shortcuts." You may choose not to follow this path. There are many good resources for learning how to execute joinery to modern aesthetic standards, and you will find a few of my favorites in the Further Explorations chapter.

This chapter will introduce you to the period-correct joinery techniques needed for the projects in this book. Like the last chapter, this one starts with a brief introduction to the tools needed. It then progresses to the techniques you will need. As with anything, practice is the key. If you don't achieve your goals at first, keep trying. You will steadily pick up the muscle memory and subtle knowledge needed to make these joints successfully by hand.

Tools of the trade

To cut period-correct joinery, in addition to the tools for preparing stock, you will need a small variety of backsaws, chisels and planes. I'll cover their basic use below, and provide more specific information throughout the construction chapters.

Cutting joinery usually starts with sawing straight, accurate lines. And that calls for a backsaw. These saws come in a variety of lengths, depths and tooth configu-

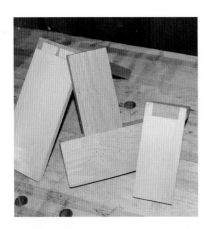

My crosscut backsaws, a 12" model and a 14" version.

Some of my backsaws, from top: a large 18" rip-filed tenon saw, a 16" tenon saw and a 14" carcass saw.

My dovetail saws, from top: the Lie-Nielsen thin-plate dovetail saw, and a saw I made from the Gramercy dovetail saw kit.

rations, but their defining characteristic is a brass or steel spine that stiffens the blade.

For the joinery in this book you will need, at a minimum, a roughly 10"-long dovetail saw, a 14" crosscut backsaw, and a 16" rip backsaw, usually referred to as a tenon saw.

A set of bench chisels is next. Handplanes get all the glory with the collectors and high-end tool makers, but the period furniture maker earns his keep with the humble chisel. Chisels are used for everything from layout to scraping glue off a surface, as well as cutting joinery of course.

Period joiners and cabinetmakers relied most heavily on square-sided chisels called firmers. They are widely available on the used and antique market but have largely been ignored by toolmakers. I prefer this style and use them in my own work. However, the bevel-edged chisel has become the standard and is more commonly available if you wish to buy new tools. Either will work well. By the way, don't listen to those who say you need bevel-edge chisels to cut dovetails. With a little skill, you can easily make square-sided chisels cut beautiful dovetails. After all, how do you think the period makers did it?

To complete the projects in this book, I recommend, at a minimum, the following sizes of bench chisels: $\frac{1}{8}$", $\frac{1}{4}$", $\frac{3}{8}$", $\frac{1}{2}$", $\frac{3}{4}$" and 1". You will also need $\frac{5}{16}$"- and $\frac{3}{8}$"-wide mortising chisels, which are discussed later in this chapter. To complete your chisel set, I'd recommend at least one long, thin paring chisel approximately $\frac{1}{2}$" wide. This will be invaluable for final fitting.

My favorite type of bench chisel, the square-sided firmer.

The difference between the traditional firmer and a modern bevel-edge chisel is obvious. The bevel-edge model has sharp edges designed to let the user work into tighter corners.

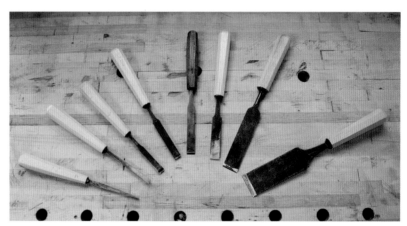

My set of square sided firmers, with shop-made octagonal handles. These chisels are the most commonly used tools in my shop.

A closeup of the chisel sides. The bevel-edge chisel is easier to use for joinery but is anachronistic to the period.

A few specialty chisels are very helpful: from top, a modern ⅜" "pigsticker" mortise chisel, a vintage ⁵⁄₁₆" "pigsticker," and a vintage ⅜" paring chisel.

In addition to the bench planes you need to prepare stock, you will need a few joinery planes. These cut shoulders and grooves at specific distances from edges and to specific depths. Some have fences and stops for that purpose and some don't.

To complete the work in this book, you will need at least: a plow plane with ¼" and ⅜" cutters, a shoulder plane, a ¾" rabbet plane, a ⅜" dado plane, a router plane and a moving fillister plane. All are available both used and new, and in multiple styles. However, as with virtually every woodworking tool, having a sharp cutter is the key to success.

Tricks for edge joints

Edge joints, and rabbets too, can barely be classified as joints, since they offer no mechanical interlock and rely solely on glue and/or nails to stay together. However, they are extremely common in all forms of furniture, not just period work, so it is important to learn how best to make and use them.

The edge joint is a simple butt joint of two square edges, used to bring two boards together along the grain. It is used most commonly to glue narrow boards together to make a wider board. The key to success is to ensure that the boards are both perfectly flat, with

My 18th-century Gabriel plow plane with full set of eight irons.

The large Lie-Nielsen shoulder plane, top, and a vintage gunmetal-infill shoulder plane. Both work exceptionally well.

Rabbet planes, both skew and straight. The skew planes work well across the grain but are more difficult to steer in general.

Dado planes. The nicker in front of blade severs the grain at the edge of the dado, and enables the tool to cut cleanly.

Router planes. A vintage beech "old woman's tooth" router and a modern Lie-Nielsen large router.

This plane is "boxed," meaning that a piece of hard boxwood is dovetailed in to prevent the working edges from wearing out. Also note the dark thumbprint, which reveals how a past user held the plane. I am careful to preserve this piece of history.

The moving fillister plane. With its nicker, depth stop and moveable fence, this plane is unmatched at cutting precise, repeatable rabbets, both with and across the grain.

perfectly square and straight edges. Any deviation from this will show as a dark line in the joint, which not only means the glue joint is weaker there but may even lead to failure.

My method for making an edge joint is to flatten one face of each board and then clamp the two boards together on edge with the flattened faces against each other (**Photo 1**), and the two edges to be glued facing up, and aligned with each other as closely as possible (**Photos 2, 3**). I then place the assembly in my face vise and plane them together as if they were one wide board, using the techniques described in the previous chapter on stock preparation.

By clamping the boards together this way, any variation from square will be canceled out when the boards are unclamped and arranged side by side (**Photo 4**). So if you are careful to produce an edge that is

1

Chalk Xs show the faces to be clamped together to make this glue joint.

2

Jointing the edges of the boards. A plane set to take a fine shaving will make a very tight joint.

3

Springing the joint, by taking an extra shaving or two in the center of the board, helps to ensure the joint is tight on each end.

4

When clamped and glued, the joint closes up nicely.

straight down its length, this technique will yield an excellent glue joint.

Once the glue dries and you've removed the clamps, prepare the unplaned side of the panel to whatever level the project requires.

Three ways to cut rabbet joints

While rabbet joints are used commonly to attach case fronts and backs in period work, they show up in other places too. In pieces from the 17th century and earlier, such as the Mannerist dresser in Chapter 3, drawer fronts often are rabbeted and the drawer sides simply nailed into that rabbet. Later, in the early 18th century, drawer sides were rabbeted to hold the drawer bottoms.

The bottoms are typically nailed or glued into the rabbets and then covered by a thin piece of wood called a drawer slip, which provides a long-lasting surface for the drawer to run on.

Rabbets can be produced in several different ways, but all methods start by laying them out with the marking gauge and ruler (**Photo 5**). How you remove the wood from there is dependent on your tool kit, your skill and your preferences. You can chisel to your lines. (**Photo 6**). You can also use the rabbet plane to cut to the lines, using your fingers as a fence (**Photo 7**).

Perhaps the most reliable way to achieve a square rabbet is to use the moving fillister plane (**Photo 8**). When using this and all other fenced tools, it is impor-

5

Proper layout for a rabbet joint. To help prevent errors, I like to mark the wood to be removed.

6

A rabbet can be cut quickly and efficiently with a chisel. Keep both hands behind the cutting edge or you run the risk of having a very bad day.

7

The rabbet can also be cut with the rabbet plane using your fingers as a fence, as shown. This tool also cleans up rabbets cut with a chisel.

8

Although designed to cut across the grain, the moving fillister plane makes cutting rabbet joints quick, easy and repeatable, due to its movable fence and depth stop.

tant that your left hand only push the tool's fence into the reference edge, and that your right hand only push the tool straight forward and down into the work. If you attempt to "steer" the tool with the right hand or push the tool forward with your left, you almost certainly will fail to cut a square rabbet.

A word on miters

A miter joint involves cutting the mating ends of two workpieces at the same angle, usually though not always 45°, to make a bend, usually 90°. Miter joints are almost completely made of end grain and will not form a strong glue bond without the introduction of a spline. So for the projects in this book, we will use miters only on decorative mouldings, where the joint doesn't have to be strong but simply requires a good fit for aesthetic purposes.

To make miters successfully, one must have the ability to cut the pieces at very precise angles. A period woodworker would have made do with a shop-made miter box as shown in **Photo 9**. This is my method as well. But if you already have a commercially made miter box for these cuts, feel free to use it (**Photo 10**).

Plow plane makes short work of grooves

Grooves run parallel to the grain, along the length of a board, while dados run across the grain. A plow plane is the best tool for most grooves. There are a number of different types of plow planes and they are commonly available both new and used.

Plowing a groove is made easier by marking out the groove first with a mortise or marking gauge. This severs the fibers at the edges and prevents them from tearing upward, but more importantly it provides a visual reference so you'll notice right away if your plow plane's fence slips, resulting in a skewed groove. Of course, the fence of the plow plane should only be run against a reference surface.

As was the case with the moving fillister, it is important that you use each hand appropriately to produce square work. Your left hand pushes the fence of the tool tightly against the reference edge, and your right hand must only push the tool forward and down into the cut (**Photo 11**). If you attempt to steer the plane with your right hand or to push the plane forward with your left, your work will be the worse for it.

9

My ugly, yet functional, miter "box," which is simply cut into my sticking board (a work-holder for making mouldings).

10

A commercially made miter box. This is probably only slightly more accurate than my simple shop-made version.

11

The plow plane in action. Remember that on any fenced plane, each hand has a separate job: The right hand pushes the plane forward while the left hand pushes the fence into the work.

12

Rather than measure, I like to use my chisels as gauge blocks to lay out joinery. This is both accurate and repeatable.

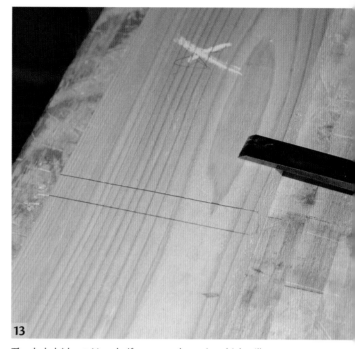

13

The dado laid out. Use a knife to score the grain, which will not only help prevent blowout but also give you a positive reference for the chisel when notching the sides of the dado (see Photo 15).

Dados, standard and stopped

Dados are most commonly used on both sides of a case to hold a shelf or cross-member of some kind. So they should always be cut on both sides at the same time, to ensure good alignment and minimize errors. Start your layout by clamping the case sides together, inside face to inside face, with the ends and edges aligned. Mark the locations for the top edges for each dado. Then using a square, pencil each mark across the front edge. I use pencil at this point because it is easy to erase if you don't like the layout.

Now pick a chisel equal to the desired dado width and use it as a measuring tool to mark the bottom edge of each dado (**Photo 12**). This is a simple way to minimize measurement errors. Use your square and pencil again to finish marking the bottom-edge lines across the reference edge.

To carry the dado layout across the inside faces of the case sides, lay each board on the bench (**Photo 13**). Using a square with a blade long enough to reach across the case side, carry the layout lines from the front edge across the entire side. Use pencil at first until you are sure you have carried the lines squarely across the case side. Then use the marking knife to mark the same line, with a light touch, giving yourself a clean line to cut to.

If you are sure your lines are where you want them, deepen them to roughly $\frac{1}{32}$" with several passes, rather than one deep cut. To complete your layout, set a marking gauge to the proper depth and scribe that depth onto both edges, front and back (**Photo 14**). Then, finish up by taking your square and marking knife and carrying those scribed lines down to meet the depth line. Another technique is to set a router plane to the proper depth, then mark the depth with that tool, using the blade as the marker, and then use the same router plane to remove the waste to the final depth.

With the layout complete and the lines struck deeply with a knife, your next step is to grab a wide, sharp paring chisel. Starting between $\frac{1}{16}$" and $\frac{1}{8}$" on the waste side of the line, pare small bevels in the waste across the full width of the workpiece. Do this on each side of the dado. The chisel will cut to the deeply struck line, lifting out chips and creating a small shoulder (**Photo 15**), which will guide your saw in the next step. Push gently, by the way, so you don't push past the scribed

14

Mark the depth with the marking gauge, darkening the knife line with a pencil.

15

Using my marking knife, I deepen the lines at the edges of the dado, and then I use a chisel to pare out chips along the inside edges of both lines. This creates a small shoulder along the inside of each line.

Use the shoulder to guide your crosscut saw.

16

line and chip out the good wood on the other side. That would leave an unsightly gap in your joinery.

Once you have beveled the waste on each line, it is time to make some saw cuts. Depending on the width of your workpiece, the 14" crosscut backsaw will usually be adequate. Larger projects could require a longer saw. If your saw spans the width of your case side, you can rely on the small shoulders you made to guide the saw

(**Photo 16**). If your saw is a little short, or if cutting freehand makes you uncomfortable, you can clamp a straightedge to the board and use it as a fence to guide your saw. In either case, make your cuts down to the depth you marked out in the layout step, paying careful attention to the depth marked on both the front and back edges. It is very easy to cut too deep, which will show in the finished piece.

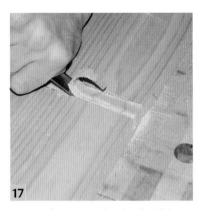

17

Remove the waste with a chisel, with its bevel facing down. Paring cross-grain like this will allow you to take a fairly deep cut with minimal effort.

18

A paring chisel makes quick work of leveling the dado bottom.

Once the sides of the dado are cut, it is a simple matter to remove the waste. I use a standard bench chisel, bevel down, to remove most of the wood (**Photo 17**). I then use a very sharp and very thin paring chisel, bevel up as much as possible, as I get close to the line, working in from both ends of the dado (**Photo 18**).

I work inward from both ends for a few reasons. One, my chisel sometimes isn't long enough to reach across the whole dado. Secondly, I don't want to blow out the back edge anyway. And third, the visible ends of the dado are what matter most, so it's OK to overcut the middle a little bit for clearance.

If you do need a perfectly smooth, level dado bottom, use a router plane for this final step (**Photo 19**). But remove as much waste as possible with a chisel first, saving the router plane for a few final thin cuts. Think of the chisel as your jack plane, and the router plane as your jointer and smooth plane.

Despite the fact that less wood is removed, stopped dados take more time to make. The layout steps are the same, with the added step of scribing a termination line on the inside face of the board, using a marking or panel gauge.

A saw is still used to cut the edges of the dado and free most of the waste, but you have to avoid scarring the wood past the termination point if that surface will be seen (**Photo 20**). Consequently, I rely more heavily on chisel work for stopped dados, especially near that stopping point. Be careful when paring the square end of the dado, since your chisel is aligned with the grain and could split it. Don't chop, using a mallet, but use

19

The router plane finishes the dado and ensures a perfectly square bottom.

20

Short strokes with the saw let you angle the toe down and reach into the end of the dado to free most of the waste.

My two favorite mallets: my shop-made joiners mallet (I call it Mjolnir) and a very heavy round mallet turned for me by my friend, Dave Bridges.

21

only your body weight to power the chisel, making a series of light paring cuts back toward the line.

The router plane is the key tool for a stopped dado, as it is the easiest way to work the bottom of the dado to the appropriate depth when you can't work inward from both ends with your paring chisel.

A basic mortise-and-tenon

Mortise-and-tenon joinery is found throughout all periods of furniture making, and therefore is a fundamental skill to learn. The basic mortise-and-tenon is quite simple to execute provided you have the proper tools – most importantly a strong chisel called a mortising chisel. You'll also need a strong mallet to drive that chisel (**Photo 21**), as well as the basic measuring tools described earlier.

The mortise is almost always cut first in furniture-making, and then the tenon cut to fit it. To make the strongest possible joint, the mortise should typically be approximately ⅓ of the width of the stock being mortised (**Photo 22**). The precise width of the mortise, however, is dictated by the chisel you have available. A ⁵⁄₁₆" chisel is probably the most versatile, as it will work for joints in stock from ¾" to 1⅛" thick. A ⅜" chisel is also useful, as you'll see later in the book.

The mortise should be cut into a squared reference surface, with its location measured from the other reference surface. To begin, set the teeth of your mortising gauge to the width of your mortise chisel. Then set the distance between the fence and the first tooth to the proper distance, again roughly ⅓ of the width of the

22

Lay out the ends of the mortise by "striking in" with the mortising chisel.

piece. Run the fence against the reference surface and scribe the mortise width, lightly at first, by pushing the gauge away from you (**Photo 23**).

Next, I take the piece of stock to be tenoned and place it in the proper position on the piece to be mortised. That helps me locate the ends of the tenon and thus establish the length of the mortise (**Photo 24**). Then I pick up the gauge again and deepen the mortise lines between the pencil marks.

Without changing the setting on the mortising gauge, take a moment to scribe the tenon on the mating piece, running the fence against the reference face (**Photo 25**). With a mortise-and-tenon, unlike some other joinery, the reference faces are usually the front or top surfaces – the ones that you want to end up flush in the final joint. At this time, you can also scribe the tenon shoulders, which define the length of the tenon itself. I like to do this using a chisel as a gauge block (**Photos 26-28**).

Back to the mortise. Place the piece to be mortised on the bench and clamp it down over a leg. You will be applying strong force with the chisel and mallet and you don't want the piece bouncing or sliding around.

Start chopping in the middle of the mortise (**Photo 29**). Orient the chisel so it's square to the face you are driving it into. I start with the bevel facing the center of the mortise and then tilt the handle down so that

The edges of the mortise are laid out with the mortise gauge (lines darkened by pencil for clarity).

The final mortise layout, showing the outline of the tenoned piece. The pencil shading makes sure I chop in the right location.

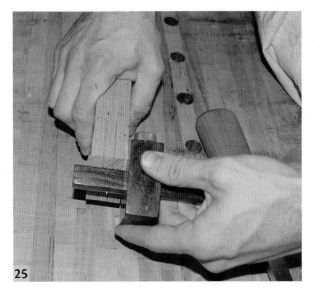

25

Lay out the tenon using the same mortise-gauge setting.

26

The length of the tenon is marked using a chisel as a gauge block.

27

Scribe a sharp line to mark out the tenon shoulder.

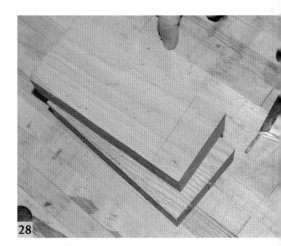

28

The scribed line, ready for the next step.

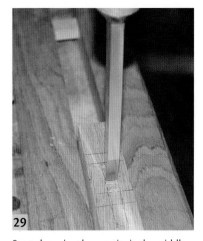

29

Start chopping the mortise in the middle.

the bevel is perpendicular before striking the chisel with a mallet.

Stay away from the ends of the mortise. Keep chipping out waste, working your way progressively deeper until you reach the final depth (**Photo 30**). Your last blows should remove the waste right up to the lines at the ends, ensuring that those edges are pristine and square (**Photo 31**).

With the mortise done, you can cut the tenon. I like to saw the shoulders with a crosscut backsaw first, and then, if the wood is straight-grained, simply split off the tenon ends and cheeks with a chisel, finishing close to the line (**Photo 32-36**). If the wood won't allow you to split away the cheeks, simply saw close to the line with a rip-filed backsaw.

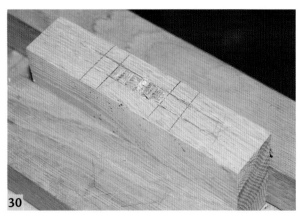

30

The mortise chopped, with a small amount of waste to remove at each end.

31

The final cuts remove the waste at the ends of the mortise, ensuring square and undamaged surfaces there, which is important on through mortises, though less so on mortises like this.

32

Saw the tenon shoulders with a crosscut backsaw.

33 Split the tenon haunches leaving a small amount of waste to pare when fitting the tenon.

34 The split completed. Avoid driving the chisel into the shoulder, as you will scar the show face of the board.

35 You can also split the waste from the tenon cheeks, as shown, if the wood is amenable. Otherwise, saw them with a rip backsaw.

36 This tenon is ready for final fitting. I left a little less than 1/16" to remove with the chisel.

37

Cleaning up and fitting the tenon with a paring chisel.

38

If you've done your job well, the reference faces of the two workpieces will wind up flush.

To smooth the tenon cheeks, you can either pare them down to the line with a chisel, plane them with a shoulder plane, or use the router plane by running the plane's base on your reference face (**Photo 37**). Test the fit of the tenon frequently while bringing it down to size. The most important element is the front face of the tenon as that dictates whether the joint will end up flush or not (**Photo 38**).

With the cheeks done, you can insert the tenon and check the fit of the shoulders. In most cases, you can undercut the shoulder at a slight angle so that the front (show) edge is the only part that touches the mortised piece, ensuring there are no gaps where they would be most visible (**Photos 39-40**).

Dovetail joints: strong but not perfect

More ink has been spilled about dovetail joints than any other woodworking topic. To some they are seen as the hallmark of fine furniture. To others, myself included, they are simply the strongest and most durable way to join the ends of two boards at a right angle. The mechanical interlock means that the joint is likely to stay together even if the glue should fail over time. So, while I'm not ready to proclaim dovetails to be the Holy Grail of woodworking, I will say it's essential that any prospective craftsman learn how to execute this joint in a functional and efficient manner.

Today, many woodworkers see dovetails as a decorative feature, but in period furniture, they were often covered up with mouldings. Both then and now, the stock in trade of a competent cabinetmaker is to be able to make dovetails of acceptable quality with speed and efficiency. Even the great makers of the past, such

39

Here, the undercut on the rear shoulder is visible. This helps ensure a tight fit on the show face with minimal effort.

40

The shoulder is tight on the show face.

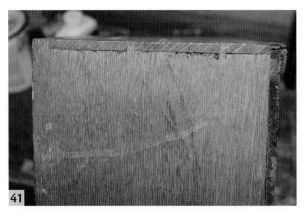

41

The back of the c.1770 drawer. Notice the ragged chisel work on the baseline of this otherwise fine piece of furniture.

42

The drawer sides show over-cuts. I interpret this as evidence of gang-sawing the sides, meaning that the dovetails were sawed in both sides at once. I think the original maker just missed his baseline!

as the Townsends, took shortcuts on this joint. You'll see over-cuts, poorly fitting tails and ragged baselines on drawers and casework (**Photo 41-42**). This section describes how to cut dovetails that are solid and functional but not necessarily decorative.

The projects in this book require two basic types of dovetails, through dovetails and half-blind dovetails. There are also specialty versions, but those are beyond our scope here.

Through dovetails are the standard version

This is the strongest variation of the dovetail, used to join case parts and the backs of drawers. Any successful dovetail joint begins with properly prepared stock. The pieces to be joined should be as flat and straight as you can reasonably make them. The end grain of the pieces should be planed on a shooting board so it is flat, square and clean – and so you can easily see layout marks.

There are different schools of thought, but I prefer cutting my dovetails tails first, as this allows me to gang-cut them and save a fair bit of time.

To begin, set a marking gauge to the thickness of your pin board and then scribe it onto both faces and both edges of your tail board, using the end grain as the reference surface for your gauge (**Photo 43**). Next, set the gauge to the thickness of the tail board and scribe both faces of your pin board. There is no need to scribe this line on the edges of the pin board. These lines are the baselines for the joint, and you should do your best to not cut past them with either saw or chisel. If you do, visible gaps will be the result – "flaws" that are seen commonly in period work but might be frowned upon by modern woodworkers. Do what you feel is right.

Once you have your baselines established, lay out the tails (**Photo 44**). The number of tails and the width

43

Scribe the baseline on the tail board. Use a gauge with a very sharp pin or knife to get an accurate line.

44

Laying out the tails with my shop-made gauge. When working at speed, I often saw them by eye without layout.

of each one will vary with the width of the tail board. I often lay out the spacing by eye, and encourage you to do the same. They won't be exact but the accuracy you can achieve might surprise you, and the slight variances will tell the world the joint is handmade. If you would rather measure, you can use a ruler to divide your board very quickly.

The slope, or angle, of the tails is supposed to be approximately 1:6 for softwoods and 1:8 for hardwoods, but period dovetails are all over the map. I typically follow the above guidelines unless I am making an exact reproduction. In that case I copy the angle of the original joinery.

However you choose to lay out your tails, make sure to mark the areas to be cut away. It is embarrassing and wasteful to remove a tail from the tail board. I use a simple X on the area to be removed, which I mark on both faces and on the end grain.

You are ready to cut the tails. I hold the tail board vertically in my vise and tilt the saw a little to cut the tails; other craftsmen choose to angle the board slightly so each cut is vertical (**Photo 45**). Even though it isn't necessary to stay on the waste side of the line when cutting tails, I still do so; it is good practice for cutting pins to fit, when staying on the waste side is necessary. Make sure your tail cuts are square across the end grain of the board, as anything less than a square cut will stop the joint from going together.

With the tails sawn, it's time to chisel out the waste. Some people prefer to saw out the waste with a cop-

ing saw, but I find it just as fast (and less annoying) to use a chisel.

Pick a chisel that will fit into your dovetails, and start by lightly tapping it into the baseline on the inside face, to deepen that line. Then pare out a small sliver of the wood by moving the chisel about $\frac{1}{16}$" away from the baseline and pushing it into the face of the board. Make one more light chop and paring cut to deepen the baseline. Don't chop down hard at the line or the wedging action of the chisel will push the baseline backward.

Now you can begin to chop out the waste. Place the chisel about $\frac{1}{8}$" away from the baseline, angle it just slightly forward of vertical, and strike it with your mallet. Now tilt the chisel forward and pare out a chip. Repeat this process, staying away from the baseline, until you've cut halfway through your board, and then flip the board over and repeat the steps on the show side until you break out the last big chunk. The last step is to make vertical paring cuts back toward the baseline, with the last cut dropping into the scribed line there.

By the way, if your saw cuts were not perfectly square, correct them now with the paring chisel (**Photo 46**).

When the tails are complete, use them to mark out the pins. To position the tail board correctly over the pin board, so the layout transfer is accurate, find an parallel-sided object that is 2" to 3" tall (I sometimes use a plane, turned on its side), and then clamp the pin board vertically in your vise so its end grain is flush with the top of the object. Now slide the object back

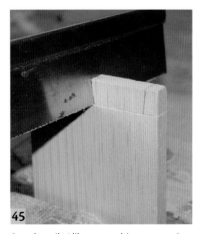

45

Saw the tails. I like to use this opportunity to practice leaving the pencil line, even though it doesn't really matter at this point.

46

Finished tails, cut and chopped. I may need to pare a little more from the left shoulder to get a good fit.

The inner face of this c.1770 drawer (side removed for repair) shows deep over-cuts along the side of each pin.

47

and use it to support the back end of your tail board, and place the front end (with the tails on it) over the end of the pin board.

Carefully line up the reference edges of the boards and make sure that the end grain of the tail board is flush with the face of the pin board. Hold it there as you mark the pins, scribing along the edges of the tails with a knife or a pencil (I use a pencil), onto the end grain of the pin board.

Now mark the waste to be removed, and then saw just on the waste side of the pencil line. Chisel out the waste as described above, and test the fit of your dovetails. Areas that are too tight can be corrected by taking light shavings with a chisel. If the fit is too loose, you can glue in shavings to tighten it up or, if the joint is still mechanically solid, you can do what many period woodworkers did: learn to live with it.

A little history on half-blind dovetails

Half-blind dovetails commonly are used at the fronts of drawers, so the dovetails are not visible on the show face. Period pieces show "flaws" and "shortcuts" on this type of dovetail as well.

A large number of 18th-century furniture pieces I have studied exhibit deep saw over-cuts on the inside face of the drawer fronts (**Photo 47**). Some of these extend an inch beyond the baseline.

Given our lack of how-to documentation from the period, my interpretation of these marks is that the makers sawed past the baseline to help release the inside corner of the waste. This practice makes waste removal nearly as simple as it is for a through dovetail.

Bear in mind that I'm a hard-core traditionalist and care very little for modern opinions and methods. Those saw cuts are evidence to me, not flaws. The men whose work I seek to understand did their jobs with speed and job-specific knowledge. The modern idea that "every surface is a show surface" is anachronistic to the period. The inside of a drawer front will seldom if ever be seen by the user, and so a period craftsman would not hesitate to over-saw a short distance in order to speed the process.

I follow this practice out of fidelity to the past. If you are doing work to suit modern aesthetics, I caution you that many will see this technique as a shortcoming. If you'd rather not cut past the baseline, you must simply spend more time chopping and paring with your chisels. Depending on the width of the tails, you may need a specialty chisel such as a fishtail chisel or a skew chisel to remove all of the waste.

Half-blind dovetails, step by step

Marking the baselines on half-blind dovetails is a little different than it is on through dovetails. For one, the drawer side and drawer front are usually two different thicknesses, and secondly, the tails stop short of the outside surface, leaving a small overlap there, usually on the front of a drawer.

Therefore, the pin board has two different baselines: one along the end grain of the board, the other on the interior face. The one on the inside face is marked out with a marking gauge set to the thickness of the drawer side. The end-grain baseline takes a little more forethought.

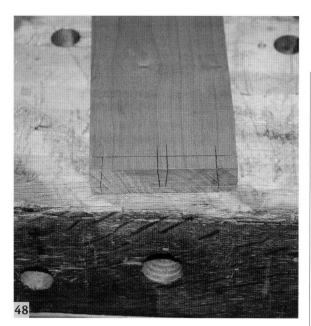

48

The pin board, on the benchtop and ready for sawing.

I like to leave at least ³⁄₁₆" (it can be a little more or less depending on the original piece) between the bottom of the tails and the front face of the drawer. If you leave less you run the risk of blowing out a chunk of the drawer front when chopping the waste.

Set the marking gauge to the thickness of the drawer front, minus the ³⁄₁₆", and scribe the line on the end grain. The same gauge setting should be used to establish the entire baseline for the tails, usually on the drawer side.

After sawing the tails and removing the waste, just as you would on a set of through dovetails, use the same setup as before to transfer the tails layout to the pins board.

To cut the pins, I use a holdfast to clamp the board to the bench, show face down (**Photo 48**). As I mentioned above, by simply over-sawing the baseline on the

Sawing well beyond the baseline makes it easy to remove the waste. Don't worry about the over-cuts – when was the last time you looked at the backside of a drawer front?

49

When chiseling the waste, I like to chop into the face and then split the waste upward by paring into the end grain and exploiting its weakness. This is fast work if you've sawed all the way down.

50

inside face of the drawer front, you can saw almost the whole pin face. To start, tilt the toe of the saw up and saw to the baseline on the end grain, at the same time sawing past the baseline on the show face by roughly ¾" or so, depending on the thickness of the board (**Photo 49**). Then you can level the saw out and take shorter strokes with the toe of the saw, digging into the inside corner to release all of the waste.

Now it becomes a simple matter to chop out the waste, and you should be able to keep the pin board in the same position on the bench. I prefer to use a narrow chisel here, which breaks out the waste rapidly but with less force (**Photo 50**). Heavy blows are risky, with the thin overlap lying just below the waste. I use the same chop-and-pare technique as I do on through dovetails. Once you have most of the waste chiseled out, clamp the board vertically in your vise. Split downward with a chisel to remove the last chunks of waste, leaving just a bit of wood to pare down to the lines (**Photo 51**). A couple of final paring cuts and you should have a finished pins socket. If the fit hangs up anywhere, pare just a bit more.

This is a fast and repeatable way to make dovetails of all kinds. And now you are ready to launch into your first real period project.

51

To remove the last bits of waste, clamp the board vertically and pare to the lines.

FURNITURE PROJECTS

CHAPTER THREE

Jacobean Chest of Drawers
c. 1700

Before I dive into the first project, chosen to introduce you to an early-American style of furniture, I'd like to dig in to the word "style" itself. As period furniture makers, we often use the word without thinking deeply about the concept.

For most of us, the word is a simple reference to shared characteristics in furniture from a certain period of time, such as Federal or William & Mary style work. However, the reality is much more complex than that. When it comes to the decorative arts, "style" encompasses not only physical characteristics but also relationships between people and where they live, as well as choices made by individual makers and their clients.

Aesthetic styles within any given period will vary widely by geography. For example, there is the incredible rococo work that was produced in Philadelphia. And sometimes groups of craftsman, such as the Goddards and Townsends of Newport, R.I., utilize similar techniques. And then there are individual choices made for specific pieces – choices about materials, levels of ornamentation and overall size. These choices were made not only by the buyer but also by the maker, as he tried to build the best piece he could while working within the constraints and conventions of his day.

While we tend to think of styles as simplistic combinations of common elements with concrete beginning and ending dates, nothing can be further from the truth. Elements were represented for years after they had gone out of fashion, and sometimes combined with other elements to create whole new styles.

So when we think about periods and styles, it's very valuable to consider the original craftsmen and the personal choices they made, given their own contexts and constraints. That will help you fully appreciate the design language of the past, and achieve the goal of accurate period reproduction.

The following chapters are predominately instructions on how to produce six pieces of furniture spanning 100 years of history, in styles popular with those seeking to make period furniture today. But I hope to inspire you to explore the circumstances of each piece's construction. Before each project, I will offer a brief history of the development of the style and its relationships to other styles. And at the end of each chapter, I will offer a few details and elements that could be changed to shift the piece from one style to another.

One final word on style. Throughout the project section, I'll use the popular nomenclature for each style, instead of terms that might be used by an art historian. For an eminent historian's perspective on the periods and terms, see Robert F. Trent's excellent Appendix at the back of this book.

Furniture in the Jacobean style

Jacobean or, more properly, Mannerist, furniture is a continuation of the high Baroque forms seen in the art, architecture and furniture of the Northern Italian Renaissance. Characterized by simple forms ornamented with applied surface decoration and strong shadow lines, Jacobean furniture came to England (and eventually her North American colonies) after the Holy Roman Empire sacked Rome in 1527. Refugees of all types, including woodworkers, fled to northern Europe and made furniture in the style they were trained in. Here in 21st-century America, we call this style "Jacobean" or "Pilgrim," referring alternately to England and the Colonies, but this ignores the furniture's true origins.

The furniture of the period was typically constructed by either a joiner (usually flat work with mortise-and-tenon joinery), or a turner (lathe-produced work such as chairs). Joiner-made furniture sometimes features applied, turned decoration, indicating an economic relationship between the two trades. The basic mortise-and-tenon joinery of the period is just like the version covered in Chapter 2.

Bright colors, turnings, inlays and multiple woods typify the decorative elements of the period. By the late 17th century, people in British North America were finally starting to feel at home in the New World; they sought fine furniture and decoration to brighten their

My painted replica of a c.1700 chest of drawers from Massachusetts. The colors are identical to those used originally, and that chest probably had a similar look when new.

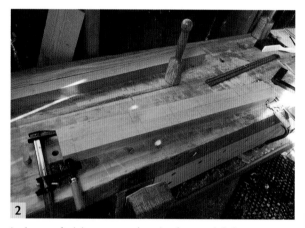

Laying out the joinery on two legs simultaneously helps to ensure that the case turns out square.

Chop the mortises after plowing the grooves. Make sure your work is held securely to the bench.

homes and showcase the wealth that was beginning to find its way into their pockets.

Building a 17th-century chest of drawers

I have chosen this chest of drawers to represent the so-called Jacobean style. It is a typical case piece of the time, made with frame-and-panel construction ornamented by elaborate moulding schemes, with side-hung drawers held together with rudimentary dovetails (some pieces of the period have rabbet and nail "joinery" instead). This piece typically would have been brightly painted and extensively decorated (see "A few finishing and construction options" on page 64 for painting instructions), but feel free to finish it naturally if the paint doesn't appeal to you (**Photo 1**). Remember that one of the goals of owning furniture was to showcase one's wealth, or at least give the appearance of prosperity. These chests were decorated either to simulate expensive pieces made with many different woods and inlays, or simply to show that the owner could afford to pay for the extra time it took to turn a simple joined piece into an elaborate work of art.

Legs then rails

This piece is made almost entirely of white oak. To begin, plane and saw the stock for the legs so they are flat and straight, using the outside faces as your reference surfaces. That done, crosscut them to final length.

The trick to a piece like this is to locate the joinery on both pairs of legs simultaneously. This will help you produce a square case. Clamp the front and rear legs together as pairs with the top ends aligned (**Photo 2**). Then lay out the vertical locations for all mortises following the dimensions given in the measured drawing. This includes the mortises for the two front rails of the case, the two rear rails, the three drawer divider rails between the front legs, and the side rails that join the front and back of the case together. At this time, you should also lay out the open-sided mortises for the (side-hung) drawer runners that attach to the front and rear legs on both sides of the case.

When you are finished laying out the mortise locations, set a mortising gauge to ⅜" (between the teeth) with the fence ⅜" away from the first tooth. Scribe the widths for all of the case mortises as well as the width of the grooves for the side and rear panels, running the gauge's fence along one of your reference surfaces. Now you can chop all of the mortises and plow the panel grooves, as described in Chapter 2 (**Photo 3**).

Use a chisel as a gauge block to lay out the tenon length. Take the chisel away to scribe the tenon shoulders all around the workpiece.

I used a numbering system, copied from the original, to keep the parts organized.

With the joints cut and grooves plowed, dry-assemble each side and check for alignment and squareness.

Dry-assemble all the joints and clamp up the case. Check for square and adjust as necessary.

With that done, prepare the stock for your four case side rails, the two front case rails, the two rear case rails, and the three drawer divider rails. Lay out and cut the tenons on each piece using the same mortising gauge setting you used to lay out the mortises. This will ensure that the rails come out flush with the legs. Use a chisel as a gauge block to lay out the tenon's shoulders (**Photo 4**). And mark which tenons go into which mortises (**Photo 5**).

With the tenons cut, fit the front and rear rails into their mortises and stand the two assemblies on your bench. Adjust the fit of the pieces until the front and rear assemblies align with each other. Once they do,

take the front assemblies apart and perform the same test with the side assemblies (**Photo 6**). Adjust until they are in alignment. The final test is to clamp up (don't glue it yet) the entire assembly and check the case for square by measuring corners, making any adjustments necessary to achieve that goal (**Photo 7**).

Make the panels and glue up the case

While the case is still clamped up, measure the openings for the side panels and the rear panel. Glue up some ¾"-thick clear white pine to the necessary width (remembering to account for the depth of the grooves and to subtract a little from the width to account for

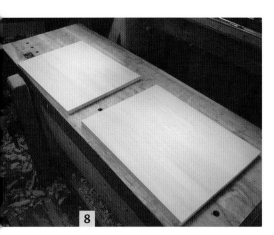

8 Start with glued-up pine panels of the appropriate width.

9 Making and fitting the panels. Don't forget these – they are sort of important.

10 Lay out the bevels using a 4"-wide piece of wood. Align one edge with the panel edge and simply run the pencil along the inside line. Do this on all four edges of both panels.

11 Planing the bevels. Plane the cross-grain parts first. That way, if you blow out the grain at the ends of the cuts, you will be able to remove the damage when planing the long-grain bevels.

seasonal movement of the panel) (**Photo 8**). The side panels should be raised, meaning that they should have a wide bevel cut along each edge to remove thickness (**Photo 9**). This is done to improve the appearance of the otherwise plain panels and also to help them fit into the ⅜"-wide grooves you plowed earlier.

To raise panels with a handplane, you need guide lines to work to. Draw lines on the face of the panel 4" away from each edge (**Photo 10**). Then use your marking gauge to scribe a line along each edge, ½" from the panel's front face.

I set a try plane for a moderate-to-fine shaving and plane down to the lines, ensuring that the bevel is flat. I usually choose the try plane because it's long enough to ensure a flat, straight bevel, and its sharp edge can put a finished surface on most boards. Start by planing

the crossgrain bevels at the ends of the panel. Those cuts can cause chipout or splintering at the back edge, but the subsequent cuts on the long-grain edges will be chipout-free and remove any of the earlier damage.

Finish each bevel with a smooth plane to ensure a smooth, flat and consistent angle from your pencil line all the way to the narrow edge of the panel (**Photo 11**). Put the assembly together temporarily to ensure that the panels seat all the way and do not hold the joinery open (**Photo 12**). Once you are sure they fit, take the assembly apart for the final time.

Now you can assemble the whole case, using glue this time. To make the assembly manageable, I like to glue each side of the case first (don't forget the panels!) and then put the two sides together with the front and rear rails. After the side assemblies are dry but before removing the clamps, bore a ⅜"-dia. hole through each of the mortise-and-tenons in the top and bottom rails (bore two in the wider bottom tenon if you like), and glue a peg in each hole.

Connect the two sides together using the front and rear rails – plus the panels, of course (**Photo 13**). When this final assembly is dry, peg the joints through the top and bottom rails as you did on the sides (**Photo 14**). Trim all of the pegs flush. By the way, you could draw-bore all of these joints and skip the glue.

Make and attach the case mouldings

The applied mouldings typical of this era are easy to fit and attach, but there are many feet of them. A bold moulding runs around the top and bottom of the case (**Photos 15-16**). Other mouldings run around the inside

12

After chopping the mortises, fitting the tenons, plowing the grooves, and raising the panels, dry-assemble the parts to be sure everything comes together properly.

13

Glue up the case in stages, sides first. Then connect them with the front and back components.

14

During each stage of the glue-up, once the glue is dry but before removing the clamps, bore through the joints and peg them.

15

16

Glue and nail the top and bottom mouldings to the case.

The D-moulding that outlines the drawer openings is mitered and then nailed to the case. Also visible is the open mortise for the drawer runner.

When mitering the side-panel mouldings, it's important that they are square. Any variation from perfection will be obvious and shoddy looking.

edges of the side paneling, and there is a D-moulding nailed around the drawer openings (**Photos 17-18**).

As for making the mouldings themselves, a few words. The slight imperfections in a hand-cut moulding are vital to the overall composition of a handmade piece of furniture. However, because the moulding isn't guaranteed to be uniform along its length, it's important that the mitered pieces be cut in order from one continuous length of moulding stock. This ensures that the profile will be similar on adjacent pieces, preventing obvious discrepancies at the joints.

For each run of moulding, select a piece of straight-grained stock that is long enough to contain all of the pieces. Joint the edge of this stock straight and square to its reference face. Then use a marking gauge to lay out the width, but leave the board wide until you are done cutting, or "sticking," the moulding.

Next I grab a moulding plane of the proper profile. There are hundreds, perhaps thousands, of different profiles to choose from, but a few simple profiles can be combined to make complex mouldings like those required for this chest of drawers.

Take a look at the toe (front end) of your plane. Most complex moulding planes operate at a "spring angle," meaning that they are held at an angle other than square when cutting. The toe of the plane should have this angle scribed on it.

Starting at the far end of the board and taking great care to keep the spring angle parallel to the reference surface, begin to stick the moulding, using short strokes at first, at the far end of the stock. I then work the moulding backwards along the length of the board, taking great care to maintain the orientation of the plane.

As with all fenced planes, each hand has a separate job here. Assuming you work right-handed, your right hand is intended to push the plane forward while your left hand pushes the plane's fence into the edge of the board. While you should sight the spring angle of the plane periodically, pushing the fence of the plane into the edge with your left hand will usually encourage the plane to maintain the right angle. Holding the plane at the proper angle also ensures that the plane will hit its integral depth stop and stop cutting once the profile is complete.

On the other hand, it's very easy to tilt a moulding plane away from its proper spring angle in an unconscious effort to keep the plane cutting. This ruins the profile, so pay attention to that spring angle and what your hands are doing.

Once the depth stop bottoms out on the board's surface, the moulding profile is complete. Now you can remove the moulding from the "mother board" using a ripsaw. Clean up the sawn edge with a finely set plane, and you're ready to miter the pieces, and glue and nail them in place. Fine cut nails are period-correct for attaching mouldings, so don't hesitate to use them (**Photo 19**).

Make and attach the top

Once you have the mouldings installed, you can make the top board for the case. Since these were usually painted, pine was the traditional material of choice. However, if you aren't going to paint the piece and the look of stained pine doesn't satisfy your aesthetic sense, feel free to use oak. Whatever wood you use, the top should end up roughly flush with the top case mouldings and the back of the top rear rail.

19

Glue and nail the mouldings to the side panels. Use fine nails that drive in easily; the panel is easy to break if you hit it too hard.

20

The top is nailed down to the case sides and front. This allows a bit of movement and is consistent with period practice. Fill the nail holes if you must.

To get a board of sufficient width you will likely have to glue up two narrower pieces. Smooth-plane the top face, but don't hesitate to leave heavy plane marks on the bottom face. Last, plane a thumbnail moulding along the outside edges.

To install the top on the case, simply predrill it for cut nails (just like the originals), and nail it on (**Photo 20**). A top this wide will move with the seasons so don't be upset if there is a gap between the top and the case for part of the year. The nails allow a certain amount of this movement without splitting the board. You can putty the nail holes or, as in the period, simply leave them.

Choose straight or shapely feet

The original this piece is based on has particularly shapely ball feet in the front. If your turning skills aren't up to the challenge, you can simply leave the front stiles long to create the front feet. There are plenty of period originals with that arrangement. If you have a lathe and basic turning skills, check the pattern presented in the measured drawing and turn away.

To attach the turned feet, bore a ½"-dia. by 1"-deep in the center of the top of each foot. Turn the case upside down and bore a matching hole in the center of the bottom end of each front stile. Cut two lengths of ½"-dia. dowel and glue one into each of the feet. I don't like to glue the feet into the case itself as I often move my furniture and want to be able to slip them out so I don't risk damaging them. But feel free to glue them into your case if you like.

A peculiar array of drawers

This type of piece has a peculiar arrangement of drawers, characteristic of late-17th-century pieces manufactured in and around Boston. There are deep drawers on the top and bottom, and two shallow drawers stuck between.

Many of these drawer boxes were joined with rabbet and nail construction; others, like the original in question here, use coarse dovetails to hold the drawers together (**Photos 21-22**). In either case, the drawer bottom is nailed into a rabbet in the bottom of the drawer front. The drawer sides and back are cut flush with

21

The drawers are dovetailed with a single large (and quite coarse) dovetail.

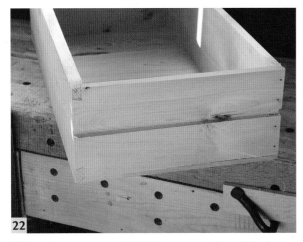

22

All four drawers are assembled this way: coarse dovetails in the front and nailed rabbets in the back.

23

Nail the drawer bottoms into a rabbet in the drawer front and onto the bottom edges of the drawer sides and back.

Nail the drawer runners into their mortises.

24

25

One nail at the end of each drawer runner will hold them in place yet allow them to be replaced easily if and when they wear out.

the bottom of this rabbet, so the drawer bottom can be simply nailed onto their bottom edges (**Photo 23**).

The drawers are side-hung, meaning that they have grooves cut in their sides that run on narrow sticks of wood, which are nailed into the legs on the inside of the case (**Photo 24**). The mortises for runners were cut when the rest of the joinery was cut, and now is the time to plane strips of oak to fit into them. Then predrill them and nail them into the case (**Photo 25**). Don't glue them in, as you want to be able to replace them easily should they wear out or be damaged over the working life of the piece.

Due to the wearing action of the runners on the grooves, drawers of this period are often made with oak. Today, this seems like a waste of an expensive material. I will illustrate with oak here for period correctness, but feel free to substitute a less expensive (but still tough) wood such as birch for your drawer sides.

I like to make the drawer-front blanks first, sizing them to fit the case openings, and then cut the rabbet for the drawer bottom (**Photo 26**). With that done, you can fit the fronts into the case and easily scribe the location of the drawer runners onto them. These marks can then be transferred to the drawer sides, enabling you to plow grooves that engage the runner in exactly the right location (**Photo 27**). Before joining the drawers, test the fit of each side on the runner and adjust as necessary to ensure smooth action.

26

Rabbeting the drawer front.

27

Plowing the side grooves in the right location is vital to ensuring a smooth-operating drawer.

Wide mouldings will be applied to decorate the drawer fronts, hiding the dovetails in front. So we can just use two coarse through-dovetails to make the drawer. Lay out and cut the joints as outlined in the chapter on joinery (**Photo 28**).

Forget – for a few minutes anyway – everything you know about producing aesthetically perfect dovetails and focus on what was done in the period in which you are working. Coarse, gappy, quickly-cut dovetails were par for the course. Join the fronts and backs to the sides for all four drawers. Glue them up, nail on the drawer bottoms, and then test the fit of each in its opening. Make any necessary adjustments for fit and sliding action but remember that the term "piston fit" is a modern creation and doesn't belong anywhere near 17th-century furniture.

With four drawers that fit and operate as they should, it is time to make the front mouldings for the drawers. Typically these would be made from an easily worked wood like pine, as I've done here, since everything would be covered with paint. But if you aren't painting the piece, you might prefer to use oak. No harm done if you do; just know that the mouldings will be more difficult to cut.

The beveled mouldings that surround the two deep drawers are made by planing a piece to approximately 2" wide by ¾" thick, and then scribing a line ½" from the reference face along one edge. Then simply bevel the piece by planing a consistent angle much in the same way you raised the side panels. The goal is to reach the line and the far edge of the face at the same time.

With that done, miter the pieces to make two simulated drawers on each deep drawer, separated by a 1½"-wide by ¾"-thick vertical piece of wood, as shown in the pictures and measured drawing (**Photo 29**). The bevels should slope down towards the outside edges of the drawer front.

Inside these beveled mouldings goes a smaller but more complex moulding, creating a smaller simulated drawer front. On period originals, these would have been painted in a contrasting color to showcase the amount of work needed to create them; here they are simply stained to match the rest of the case. Again, ensure that you make enough moulding in one run to complete each drawer front; you want to make sure the profile is consistent from piece to piece (**Photo 30**).

Complete and attach the drawer mouldings, and then, using the same moulding profile, make the moulded squares that are brad-nailed onto the raised

28

The bevel mouldings on the drawer front turn the through dovetails into half-blinds.

29

On the drawer fronts, wide bevel mouldings flank a small ovolo moulding on the inside. Nails and glue hold everything in place.

side panels. Then give yourself a pat on the back, as this completes the woodwork for the project (**Photo 31**).

A few finishing and construction options

As mentioned earlier, many of these late 17th-century chests of drawers were painted wildly. Polychromatic paint schemes, plus simulated inlay and grain-work, were the order of the day. However, in centuries since they were made, many of these pieces suffered the indignity of being stripped by their owners, in order to match the misguided idea that the period was a very dark and boring place.

My painted version of this chest is based on chemical analysis of a piece in the Metropolitan Museum of

Art, and you can choose to paint your piece in a similar fashion, or you can simply stain the piece to unite the woods and give the appearance of age. But I hope you will at least consider the paint route. Whichever you choose, apply the finish before attaching the drawer pulls and escutcheons.

Another period-correct option is to leave the front legs long instead of adding the ball feet. It is a safe bet that some pieces had straight front legs because there are signs of them being cut off to add ball feet later. The evidence is open mortise-and-tenon joints where the lower case rails meet the legs. It wouldn't have made sense to leave them open so the theory is that the legs were cut off after the fact. There is no way to prove which is correct, so do what you feel looks best.

And last, this type of Jacobean construction can easily be adapted to many different forms. Blanket chests, chests-over-drawers, and even chairs can be made with a few dimensional modifications. For inspiration, see the work of Peter Follansbee.

30

A sticking board makes it easier to plane mouldings from narrower pieces of wood.

31

The shadows from natural light showcase the mouldings better than any photography light.

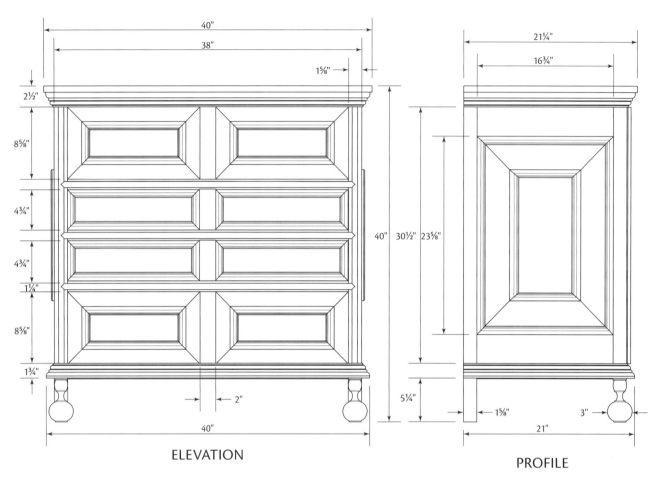

ELEVATION

PROFILE

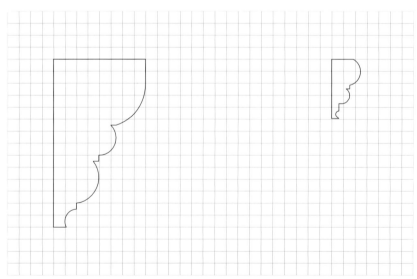

MOULDING PROFILES
One square = ⅛"

JACOBEAN CHEST OF DRAWERS

OVERALL DIMENSIONS: 21¼" DEEP X 40" WIDE X 40" TALL

Qty	Part	Dimensions (inches)			Stock	Comments
		Thickness	Width	Length		
4	Legs	1⅝	1⅝	39⁵⁄₁₆	white oak	Two front legs will be cut off eventually but start out the same length as rears
2	Case side top rails	⅞	5¼	18¼	white oak	¾" tenons both ends
2	Case side lower rails	⅞	5¼	18¼	white oak	¾" tenons both ends
2	Case side raised panels	¾	17¼	24⅛	white pine	
1	Case back top rail	⅞	5¼	36¼	white pine	¾" tenons both ends
1	Case back bottom rail	⅞	4	36¼	white pine	¾" tenons both ends
1	Case back panel	⅜	25⅝	35¼	white pine	
1	Case top	¾	21¼	40	white pine or white oak	
1	Case top moulding	1	1¾	85	white pine or white oak	
1	Case base moulding	1	1¾	85	white pine or white oak	
4	Drawer dividers	1¼	1¼	36¼	white oak	¾" tenons both ends
8	Drawer runners	¾	1¼	18¼	white pine	
2	Deep drawer fronts	¾	8⅝	34¾	white pine	
4	Deep drawer sides	¾	8¼	16¾	white pine	
2	Deep drawer backs	¾	8¼	34¼	white pine	
2	Deep drawer bottoms	⅜	16⅜	34¾	white pine	
2	Deep drawer central plaques	¼	2	8⅝	white pine	
2	Deep drawer bevel mouldings	½	1¾	55	white pine or white oak	Make in one length, miter & cut to fit
2	Deep drawer central moulding	⅜	1	40	white pine or white oak	Make in one length, miter & cut to fit
2	Shallow drawer fronts	¾	4¾	34¾	white pine	
4	Shallow drawer sides	¾	4½	16¾	white pine	
2	Shallow drawer backs	¾	4½	34¼	white pine	
2	Shallow drawer bottoms	⅜	16⅜	34¾	white pine	
2	Shallow drawer central plaques	½	2	4¾	white pine	
1	Shallow drawer moulding	⁷⁄₁₆	1	45	white pine or white oak	Make in one length, miter & cut to fit
2	Side panel moulding squares	⅜	1	135	white pine or white oak	Make in one length, miter & cut to fit
1	Drawer opening moulding	½	¾	175	white pine or white oak	Make in one length, cut to fit
2	Ball foot	3 dia.		5¼	white pine	

Note: Rough cut all parts oversize then cut to fit.

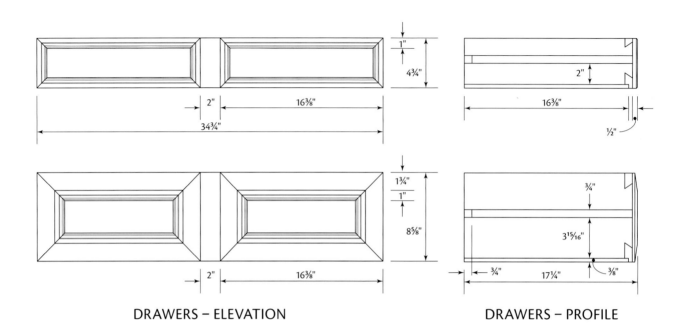

DRAWERS – ELEVATION

DRAWERS – PROFILE

DRAWERS – EXPLODED VIEW

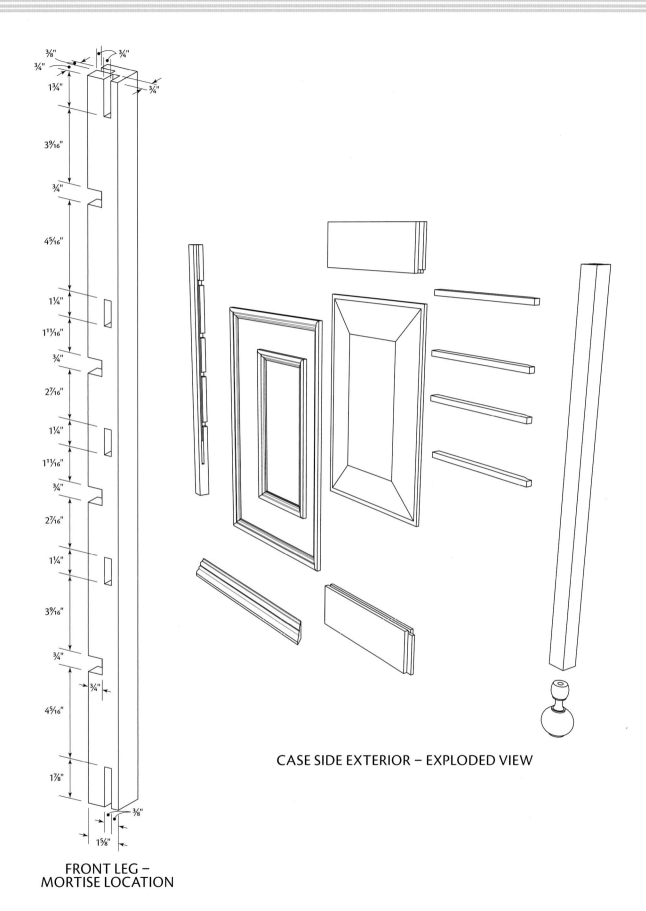

3/8"

3/4"

3/4"

3/4"

1 3/4"

3 9/16"

3/4"

4 5/16"

1 1/4"

1 11/16"

3/4"

2 7/16"

1 1/4"

1 11/16"

3/4"

2 7/16"

1 1/4"

3 9/16"

3/4"

3/4"

4 5/16"

1 7/8"

3/8"

1 5/8"

FRONT LEG –
MORTISE LOCATION

CASE SIDE EXTERIOR – EXPLODED VIEW

CHAPTER FOUR

William & Mary Chair
c. 1720

Mid-17th-century England was fraught with political and religious crises. The tumult of the English Civil War, the leadership of Oliver Cromwell, and the 1660 restoration of the monarchy under Charles II (son of the beheaded Charles I) left English citizens hungry for stability. When Charles II died in 1685, his brother James II succeeded him. However, suspicious of James II's pro-French and pro-Catholic sentiments as well as his designs on absolute power, the Protestant nobility called on Dutch stadtholder William of Orange, son of James II's sister Mary Stuart and husband to James II's daughter (also named Mary Stuart), to invade England and serve as king. William and Mary became co-regents after their successful invasion, the so-called "Glorious Revolution" of 1688.

This swath of history gives us the source of the name, William & Mary. But it doesn't explain why the furniture of the period has such a characteristic look. The answer to that question goes back to England's long-time enemy (and sometimes ally) France, and a Huguenot named Daniel Marot.

In 1598, Henry IV of France issued the Edict of Nantes. The Edict granted French Protestants, known as Huguenots, the right to live, work and worship in the otherwise Catholic nation of France. However, in 1685, Louis XIV issued the Edict of Fontainbleau, which revoked the Edict of Nantes and assured the persecution of the Huguenots. In their flight from France, Huguenot refugees found their way to all corners of the continent. A well-known example is the Fabergé family, who escaped to Russia and ultimately produced the storied Fabergé eggs for Czar Alexander.

Daniel Marot was a Huguenot who had worked as a designer at the French court. His escape took him to Holland, where he became the Court designer for William of Orange, and was largely responsible for the interiors of Het Loo, William's palace in Holland.

Marot's engravings and designs were a unique amalgamation of French style and Dutch sensibility, and captivated William and Mary. After the Glorious Revolution, Marot followed William and Mary to England. Until 1695, Marot worked in England and produced many designs for the Court, which then filtered down through the nobility and ultimately became the dominant high style of the period.

The William & Mary style generally features fairly squat proportions, especially when compared to later styles. Turned legs are common on case pieces, especially on the high chests of drawers that became the dominant case form of the time.

William & Mary was very much a transitional style between the harsh and bold Mannerist style and the optimistic and hopeful styling of Queen Anne, and our Boston chair is a good example. The caning that was common on early William & Mary seating, and on Dutch and Flemish chairs, had given way to the leather upholstery seen on the project chair. And early straight or slightly angled backs had been supplanted by the sensuous curves of our "crook'd back" chair.

In British America, William & Mary furniture was popular for a relatively short time, roughly from 1700 to 1725. It enjoyed some overlap with the Mannerist style at the turn of the 18th-century, but was replaced as the fashionable style by Queen Anne early in the 1720s. Some forms of William & Mary furniture, such as our chair, remained popular and were mass-produced into the 1740s, but the style was largely bypassed by then. Because of the cachet of the styles that came after, William & Mary has never been very popular with modern reproduction furniture makers. However, the furniture is common in English country homes to this day.

Use templates for this chair and others

As is the case with many period chairs, the building process starts with the back legs. I'm lucky enough to own an original of this chair, c.1720, which made it easy for me to trace its parts directly onto my template stock (**Photo 1**), and create the patterns in the measured drawing. I also penciled the joinery locations onto the template.

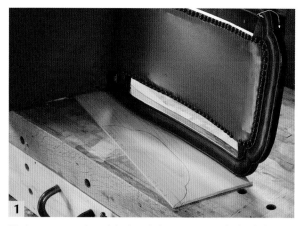

1

Having access to the original made it easy to trace the back shapes directly onto my template stock.

2

When all of the templates were done, I tacked them together to check them against the original chair.

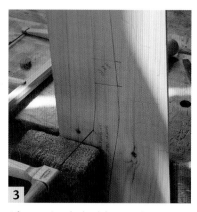

3

After tracing the back leg template onto ¼"-thick pine, I sawed carefully to the lines.

4

Planing the stock for the legs.

Since one chair is rarely enough and you will certainly want to make another someday, I recommend that you make templates for the main chair parts, to get the geometry right and record their shapes (**Photo 2**). Templates also ensure that parts match on the two sides of the chair.

This chair requires only a small amount of maple but the stock preparation is vital to the project's success – even more than it is for a case piece. Any inaccuracy in the joinery areas will lead to a chair that is out-of-square and unstable. To begin, plane a piece of 2"-thick maple flat and bring it to a final thickness of 1⅞" for the legs. Then lay out the leg template using the measured drawing, saw the template, and trace it onto the leg stock (**Photo 3**).

At this time, prepare the stock for all of the other parts of the chair. Try for a smooth surface on the parts that won't be covered with leather or shaped any further (**Photo 4**).

How to shape the legs

With the stock prepared and the curves laid out, cut close to the line with either a bowsaw or by whittling away the waste with straight cuts from a regular ripsaw (**Photo 5**). In the joinery areas, namely the lower leg, I like to use the ripsaw, which makes it easier for me to maintain a plumb cut. You will be planing this later, but it is better to start as square as possible (**Photo 6**). At this time you should also cut the curved back splats using the same template.

Take your rough leg blanks to the bench and use a compass plane to finalize the shape, working to your layout lines. The legs will come out more identical if you clamp them together for the last few compass-plane strokes, as well as some shaping with a fine rasp (**Photo 7**).

Make sure to keep the front face of each leg square to the inside face. On some chairs this junction is angled but on the original chair they are square. The final check here is to put your legs on the bench about 14"

5

When the stock is flat, lay out the rear legs. They can be nested – meaning laid out very close together on the same piece of wood – to create less waste.

6

When sawing and planing the rear legs, be sure to keep the joinery areas square and plumb.

7

After planing the curves with a compass plane, use a fine rasp to finalize the leg shape. Make sure to clamp the legs solidly together so they don't slip.

apart and use your winding sticks to make sure that the seat joinery areas are in one plane (**Photo 8**). If they are not, make the necessary adjustments until they are perfect. Accept nothing but perfection here or you will have problems down the road.

Build the back and front of the chair first

The chair is wider in the front than it is in the back. This means that the side rails join the front and rear legs at an angle, while front and rear rails are joined square. I like to start with the square joinery, assembling the back of the chair first and then the front leg assembly, before tackling the sides.

Cut the square joinery for all of the rear rails first. Align and clamp the legs together, and draw the mortise locations on both legs, using the template to tell you

8

Winding sticks are vital to ensure that the chair back turns out flat and square.

where they go. Then chop all of these square mortises to the width described in the measured drawing, and tenon and fit all of the back rails (**Photo 9**). Before taking the back of the chair apart, mark and cut the joinery that will hold the crest rail and two back splats in place (**Photos 10-14**). When you are finished, you'll be able to dry-assemble the entire back of the chair — letting you check and tweak the fit of each joint to ensure it is as tight, square and strong as possible (**Photo 15**).

With the rear assembly fit but not glued, turn your attention to the front leg assembly. Join the two front legs to the top seat rail, per the measured drawing or

With the two lower rails tenoned and dry-fit into the legs, scribe the tenon shoulders of the lower back rail.

Use a template to lay out the crest rail.

Chop the mortises in the crest rail. Make sure to leave enough "meat" on the outside edge or you risk cutting into the mortise when you shape the curves.

Scribing and cutting the crest rail tenons on the top of the rear leg.

Fit the crest rail so that the front faces are flush with each other. Also ensure that the penciled curves line up with the outside edges of the legs, and make adjustments to the lines as necessary.

Scribing the length of the back splats.

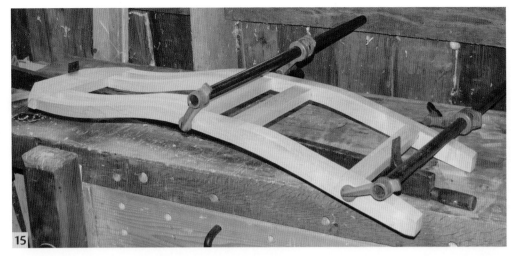

Dry-fit the completed back. Tweak the joinery as necessary to get a square assembly with a good fit at each tenon shoulder. The crest rail is only roughly shaped at this point.

Place the front-leg blanks side by side and use a template to lay out the mortise locations and the pommels (square portions of the turned leg).

The outside face of the front leg is planed at an angle. The exact angle is determined after drawing a full-size seat plan.

The front legs, planed to the proper angles. Remember that the chair is wider in the front than at the back; if you keep that in mind you will plane the angles in the right direction.

templates, if you made them, but don't glue the parts yet. Now turn the middle stretcher to the design shown in the plan, and lay out the locations of the pommels (square portions) on the front legs (**Photo 16**). Lay out a hole (to serve as a mortise for the front stretcher) in each leg, and then bore the holes. Dry assemble the front-leg assembly and check for fit and square. The outside of each leg will be planed to the seat angle before it is turned, so the next step is to figure out what that angle should be (**Photos 17-18**).

Make a full-size plan for the seat angles

With the front and rear leg assemblies dry-fit and ready for the side joinery, draw a full-size plan of the seat (**Photo 19**). I almost never work to a full-size measured drawing, but chairs are the exception in my shop. Rolls of brown paper are available in craft or office supply

19

The full-size seat plan. I usually don't draw plans but chairs are an exception.

20

The mortises for the side rails are angled. Use the full-size drawing to set the angle on the bevel gauge, and lay it on the rear legs. Make sure the angle goes the right way!

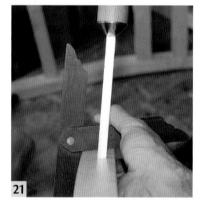

Use the bevel gauge and your eyeballs to guide the mortise chisel.

21

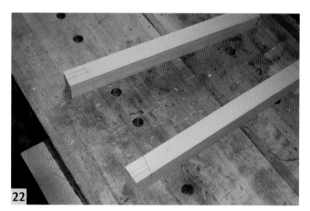

22

Angle the mortises, not the tenons. Having straight grain in the tenons, as shown here, is vital to a strong chair.

stores and make an excellent and inexpensive drawing surface for this and other shop tasks.

The drawing will prove invaluable as you attempt to cut the angled joinery for the side rails. While these chairs are admittedly much easier than later chairs to understand – these seat joints angle in only one direction, while later chairs feature compound angles – the angles will still cause you problems if you don't figure them out in advance.

Set your bevel gauge to the angle indicated by the plan. Use that bevel gauge to guide your mortise chisel as you chop the angled mortises in the front and rear legs (**Photos 20-21**). Carefully think about which way the rails will angle when you chop them or you will end up starting all over again.

It might seem easier to make angled tenons and straight mortises, but this is a bad idea. You'll end up with weak "short grain" in exactly the wrong place.

23

Cutting and trimming the seat-rail tenons. While the tenon is straight, the shoulders are angled to meet the front and rear legs.

Think about the stresses that a chair undergoes and where that force is exerted, and you will quickly understand why straight-grained tenons are superior (**Photos 22-23**).

With your angled mortises chopped and the tenons fit, dry-assemble the chair one more time to check the fit of all tenon shoulders and to make sure that all of the angles match from side to side. With the chair still dry-fit, check that the legs meet the outline drawn on the roughly shaped crest rail and make any necessary adjustments.

Now you can cut the curved outer profile of the crest rail with your bowsaw and finish to the line with rasps and scrapers, taking special care to achieve a smooth transition between the outside edges of the rear legs and the side of the rail itself (**Photos 24-25**).

Back legs have a moulded face

The final steps on the chair are decorative. Above the seat, the front surface of the rear legs is moulded. A bead is scraped along each of the front corners, and the center of the surface is shaped convex. The profile is carried seamlessly onto the crest rail.

To make the moulding, I use a profiled scraper. This is done by taking any piece of spring steel (old handsaws can be cut into blanks, or you can simply use the corner of a card scraper as I did for this project), and file a half circle about ¾" away from a corner with

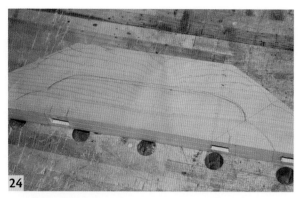

The rough-shaped crest rail.

When shaping and smoothing the outside edges of the crest rail, check the junction with the outside of the leg to ensure a smooth transition.

I made the moulding scraper from an old card scraper, using a flat file and a ⁵⁄₁₆" chainsaw file.

a ⁵⁄₁₆" chainsaw file. Relieve the remaining ¾" into an oval shape with the top of the oval being the same height as the bead – in effect the same distance from the original edge (**Photo 26**).

Note that the moulding begins an inch or so above the rear seat rail so it doesn't interfere with the seat joinery, and also so you don't bother moulding an area that will be hidden by upholstery.

A wood fence can be added to guide the scraper, or you can just freehand it like I did. To get the bead started and help to keep the scraper on track, put a wood screw into a block of scrap and use it like a marking gauge to establish the width of the bead (**Photo 27**). Before using the scraper, practice on scrap to get the cutting angle right. Then scrape the mouldings along both front edges of each rear leg, using a light touch and many shallow passes (**Photo 28**). The less material you take with each pass, the better chance you have of leaving a smooth surface.

You will have to finesse the center of the moulding to achieve a smooth convex face. To do that, use a straight scraper to smooth the edges left by the shaped scraper. Sand if necessary but make sure to stay away from the beaded edges as it's very easy to create noticeable flat spots there.

Crest-rail moulding is the real challenge

With the moulding scraped into the legs, you must now tackle the moulding of the crest rail. Believe me when I say this is the most difficult part of the build. I've been making things out of wood for over 20 years and I still ended up making three crest rails. Before beginning, it is vital that every tool you will use is as sharp as you can make it and, as Roy Underhill says, that you "clean your mind of impure thoughts."

To begin, position the crest rail on top of the legs, and transfer the locations of the beads. Next, draw smooth curves that are parallel with the outside edges of crest rail, about 2½" inboard. Using a French curve, smooth these curves and connect them to the starting points for the beads, which you transferred from the legs.

Use your marking knife and score the line you just drew. This gives you a cut to chisel into. Now pare out shallow chips along the bottom of the curve, including the area that will ultimately be covered with upholstery. Continue the knife and chisel work until you have a shallow trench that defines the bottom of the moulded area.

Now you can carry the moulding along the curved crest rail. To form the bead closest to the edge you can

27

To define the inner edge of the beads, and give the scraper a track to ride in, use a simple screw in a piece of wood.

28

The scraper creates the bead and the beginning of the curved center portion. Use a straight scraper to smooth the center area into a consistent curve.

use the same tools you used for the back legs: the block and screw, and the handheld scraper. Make sure the scraper is freshly filed and sharp before using it on the rail, as a fair portion of the scraping will be across the grain, a notoriously tricky thing to do. This is exactly where I ruined two rail blanks before getting one that was usable for the chair. I went too fast and pulled out chunks of the bead across the grain, resulting in a gap-toothed look. When that happens, there is nothing to do but start again with a new blank.

To reach the inside bead, I recommend making another small scraper that fits into a scratch stock as seen in **Photo 29**. Like the handheld scraper, it will cut the bead and also the beginning of the convex section between them. To finish fairing the center section, use a straight scraper as before. I also used sandpaper extensively on my crest rail to smooth the convex area and the bead transitions.

When you are happy with the molded areas, use a chisel to smooth the corners below it that won't be covered by upholstery. Sand these areas smooth, again taking care to avoid flat-spotting the beads. With the rail completed, test-fit it once more on the rear legs to make sure the beads flow smoothly into one another. If not, use a scraper to bring them flush to each other.

Smart approach to assembly

Because of the angles in the seat, it's best to glue up the side assemblies first (and let them dry) before joining the two sides together with all of the cross-members. If you were to do the opposite, and glue up the front and rear assemblies first, the angles in the side pieces would make any further assembly very difficult.

After each stage of the glue-up, when the glue is dry but the clamps are still on, peg every mortise and tenon joint except those on the crest rail, to ensure that they stay together for the long haul.

Once the chair is out of the clamps, go over every intersection with a handplane, making paring cuts across the grain at a 45° angle to ensure that they are smooth. Then set the chair onto its feet to make sure it isn't a rocking chair (**Photo 30**). Trim the feet as necessary.

A few finishing options

According to decorative arts scholar Robert F. Trent, a maple "crook'd back" chair like this would have originally been finished with a red wash under dark

29

The earlier tools will handle the outer bead on the crest rail, but for the inner bead I recommend a scratch stock fitted with a ⁵⁄₁₆" bead cutter.

brown shellac, designed to resemble walnut, the preferred wood of the period.

So why not just use the darker wood? I believe the reason was that walnut lacks the strength of hard maple and, in a chair with a curved back and numerous joints, strength is at a premium.

I chose to follow Mr. Trent's advice on the finish, at least approximately. The chair you see here was finished with three coats of a thinned oil-based mahogany stain. Then I tinted a 1-lb. cut of blonde shellac with Van Dyke brown dye and brushed on four coats, rubbing out the last coat with with a dark brown paste wax and 0000 steel wool.

Another finishing option, which would closely replicate a fair number of originals, is simply to paint the chair black. A number of these chairs have been painted — leather and all — over the years, perhaps as a simple refresh for an old and faded color finish. If you go this route, you might want to try a multi-layer paint job (on the wood only), applying a brighter color under the black paint and then rubbing through the black to expose the base color in areas that would see a lot of wear in use. This is done commonly on Windsor chairs.

Lessons and options

Learning to make this stout design will serve you well for any chair project. You'll learn why straight grain and tight joinery matters, and come to appreciate the extra security of good, strong split white oak pegs.

While a fully turned chair such as a Windsor obviously uses different techniques, the basic construction of this chair can be applied to almost any type of cabinetmaker-built chair. By angling the legs toward the center and tweaking the joinery accordingly, you can make a Chippendale-style chair. Changing from an upholstered back splat to a shaped splat will move this chair up 20 years or so to the Queen Anne style. Spanish feet will move the chair slightly back in time.

The assembled chair, before finishing. Note the pegs in the lower rail's mortise-and-tenon joints.

30

WILLIAM & MARY CHAIR

OVERALL DIMENSIONS: 19⁵⁄₁₆" DEEP X 20¼" WIDE X 41¾" TALL

Qty	Part	Thickness	Width	Length	Stock	Comments
		Dimensions (inches)				
1	Crest rail	1	3¾	14⅝	maple	
2	Rear legs	3⅝*	1½	38½	maple	*Gross stock dimension; ½" tenon top ends
2	Front legs	1¾	1¾	17⅜	maple	Plane to proper angles per instruction on page 75; turn leg based on illustration
2	Back splats	1⅜*	1¼	17⅜	maple	*Gross stock dimension; ½" tenon both ends
1	Lower back rail	1	1¾	12⅞	maple	⅝" tenon both ends
1	Rear seat rail	1	1¾	12⅞	maple	⅝" tenon both ends
1	Front seat rail	1¼	1¾	18¼	maple	¾" tenon both ends
2	Side seat rails	1¼	1¾	15⁹⁄₁₆	maple	¾" tenon both ends
1	Lower rear stretcher	1	1¾	13⅛	maple	¾" tenon both ends
1	Lower front stretcher			18¼	maple	¾" tenon both ends; Turn according to illustrations starting with 2" x 2" stock
2	Lower side stretchers	¾	1⅞	17⅜	maple	¾" tenon both ends

Note: Rough cut all parts oversize then cut to fit.

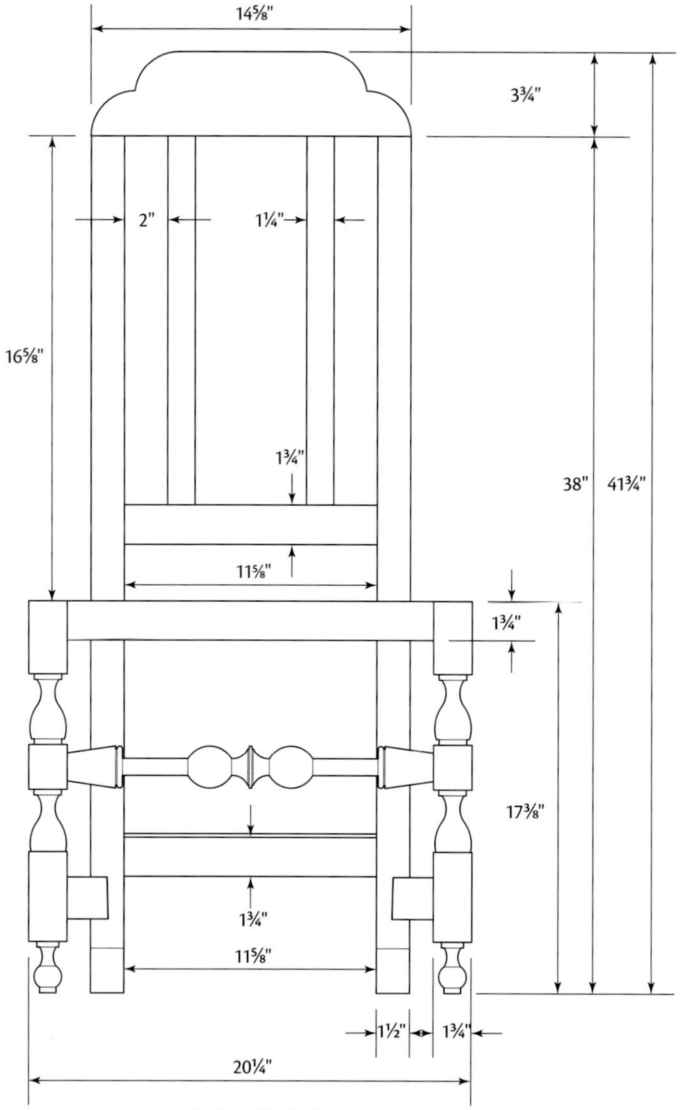

ELEVATION

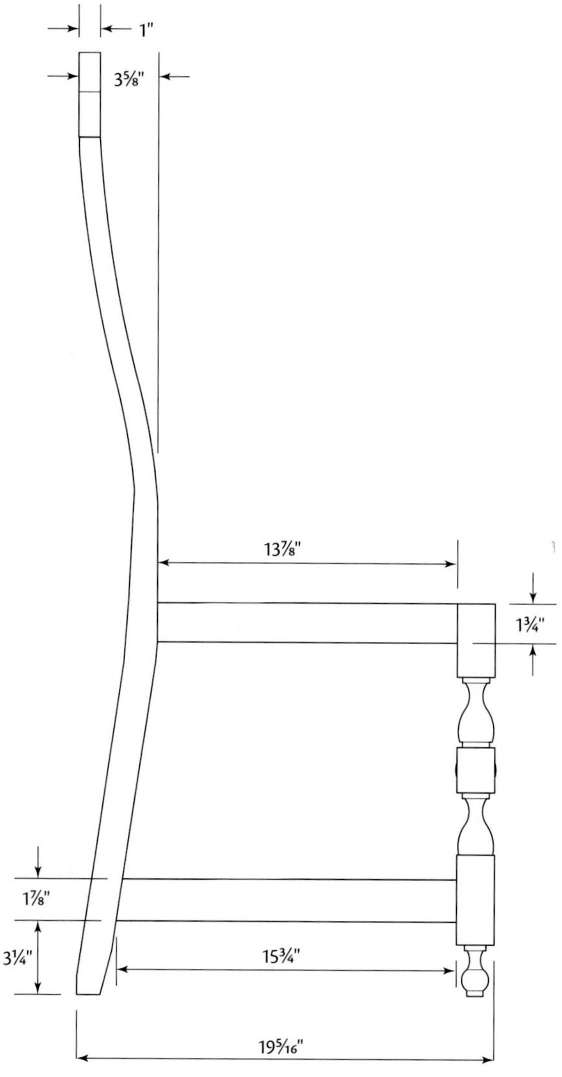

PROFILE

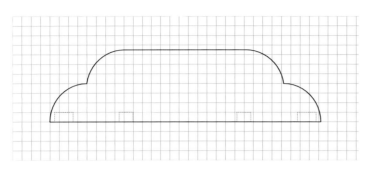

CREST RAIL PATTERN WITH MORTISES
FOR BACK SLATS & LEGS
One square = ½"

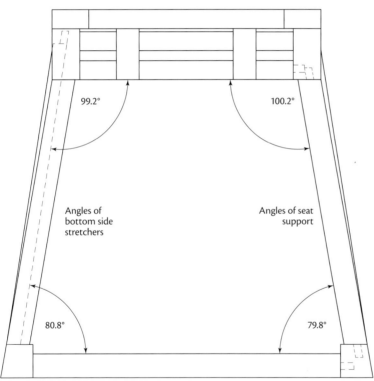

99.2°

100.2°

Angles of
bottom side
stretchers

Angles of seat
support

80.8°

79.8°

Front stretcher removed for clarity

TOP VIEW

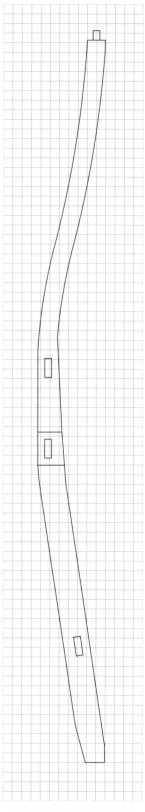

BACK LEG PATTERN
One square = ½"

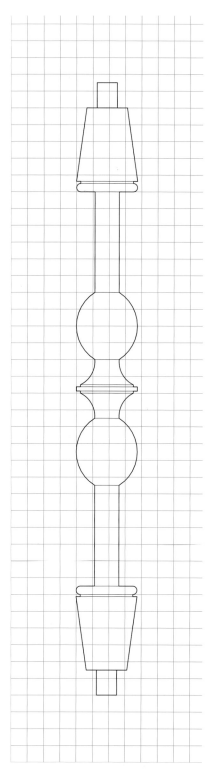

**FRONT TURNED
STRETCHER PATTERN**
One square = ½"

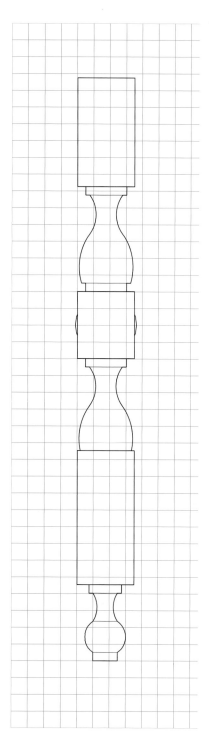

**FRONT TURNED LEG
PATTERN**
One square = ½"

Upholstering the Crook'd Back Chair

By Michael Mascelli

Boston in the mid-18th century was a bustle of commerce, immigration and innovation, including the creation of some of the most influential furniture forms in the Colonies. As London set the fashion and Mass. makers like Thos. Fitch proudly advertised that they could replicate it, chair shipments fanned out from Boston, incluencing how chairs were made and sold in other major centers like Philadelphia and New York, as well as countless smaller cities and towns.

At the same time, the art of the upholsterer was coming into its own, as a full-fledged partner in the rapidly expanding furniture trade. Colonial upholsterers played a role similar to English "upholders," acting as a sort of general contractor who coordinated the creation of all sorts of soft goods, including draperies and slip covers – and thus becoming a primary importer of fabrics and trims.

Thomas Chippendale was an upholder of period furniture design in England and the Colonies – as were many other well-known figures. One American example is Plunket Fleeson, who advertised himself as lately arrived from London and Dublin, though he was likely born in Philadelphia. Fleeson offered a full range of soft goods, including mattresses for both sailing ships and homes, and worked hard to compete with the influx of very competitively priced chairs from Boston. There was clearly a strong demand for more comfortable, stylish chairs, and a growing pool of homegrown talent to fill it.

For centuries, seating furniture could be summarized in two words: flat and hard. The common way to make a wooden chair more comfortable was to add a soft, loose pillow, which could be made easily with needle and thread, relocated to other chairs as needed, and protected from flying embers and creeping pests.

When a true "middling" class began to emerge in 16th-century England – tradesmen and merchants who could afford more comfortable furniture – the techniques of the saddle maker and coachbuilder were used to attach stuffing materials more permanently to chairs. In its most basic form, this early upholstery

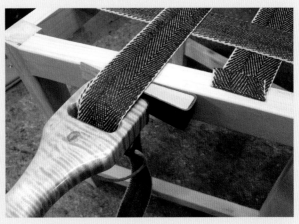

A leather-covered wedge helps the strainer on the angled sides of a seat frame.

involved placing some locally sourced material like straw, sea grass, coir fiber[1] or cattails on a solid wooden seat and covering it with a sturdy fabric – most often a plain "neat"[2] leather.

However, as the mass production of turned parts greatly reduced chair prices, upholstery methods were forced to evolve to meet the rising demand.

Finished black-and-white linen webbing.

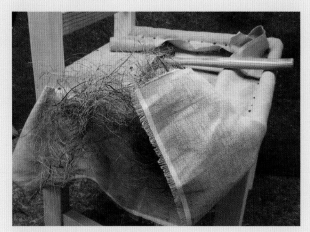
Stuffing the edge roll with coir fiber.

Completed edge roll, with bridle stitches in place.

The basic method emerges

The basic technique for upholstering an open-frame seat that developed next – around 1600 – did not fundamentally change until the introduction of modern materials in the 20th century.

A sturdy, narrow linen webbing was interwoven and stretched tightly across the frame, and then covered with a coarsely woven fabric referred to generically as hessian, sackcloth or burlap. When loose stuffing material was placed on this "deck," the upholsterer faced the challenge of keeping it in place. In some cases the stuffing was simply left loose and covered, but in the best work the upholsterer first installed loose "bridle" stitches in the deck, and then carefully placed handfuls of curled horsehair under them until the entire seat was filled.

This improved system still did not account for the extra pressure exerted on the edges, especially the front, so more innovations quickly followed – all variations on a stuffed and sewn edge roll. Upholsterers used a combination of sturdy fabric and stuffing materials, plus hand stitching, to create a strong "curb" around the frame, which better-defined the shape of the seat and also formed a well into which the loose stuffing could be placed. The choice of edge-stuffing materials ranged from stiff bulrush reeds to firm coir fiber and soft curled horsehair, with the number and style of hand stitches varying greatly from one craftsman to another.

In early seating, the height or loft of the upholstery is described as low profile or high profile. Very early pieces usually had very flat, barely padded treatments. Later and more formal pieces often had upholstery "peaks," formed by leaving the tops of the front legs taller than the rails and shaping them into gentle triangular peaks. These fixed corner points allowed the upholsterer to create an edge that was firm and tall, with crisp corners that defined the height of the upholstery. In some of these cases a "side webbing" was used, by placing webbing material on edge and wrapping the entire seat frame to form the outside of the upholstery layer. The upholsterer could then use stuffing and stitches to create an edge roll that provided the proper look for that chair.

These developments are the true beginning of a partnership between designer, joiner and upholsterer in the creation of comfortable seating, and eventually evolved much further into the very elaborate handsewn edges seen on the serpentine contours of wing chairs and camel-back couches.

Building a traditional seat foundation

The first step in any traditional upholstery treatment is to gently ease the edges of all seat-frame members with a coarse rasp, scraper or handplane, to ensure that nothing sharp will cut into the various fabric layers.

For this Boston chair, traditional English "black and white" webbing is installed, using a toggle-type stretcher (or "strainer") so as not to damage the herringbone weave of the material. Beginning on the back rail, the webbing is folded under, and secured with four webbing tacks set in an offset pattern to avoid splitting the rail. The webbing should be pulled until it is just nicely taut. Three strips of webbing are installed front to back and three side to side, in a simple over/under weave pattern.

The first stuffing is loose horsehair.

Cotton batting is placed inside the edge roll.

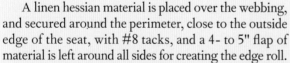

Cotton muslin or drill cloth completes the foundation, which should be firm and flat.

The show cover is folded back over itself and marked for Y-cuts.

A linen hessian material is placed over the webbing, and secured around the perimeter, close to the outside edge of the seat, with #8 tacks, and a 4- to 5" flap of material is left around all sides for creating the edge roll.

On the front and sides, loose coir fiber is shaped and placed along the edge to fill the edge roll, and then the flaps are folded back in and tacked with #8 tacks. This edge roll is then stitched by hand using a waxed linen mattress twine and two straight needles, one at either end of the twine. Working from the middle of the twine a series of saddle stitches is run along the bottom edge of the roll, and then a second line at about the middle of the edge roll to refine the shape. The goal is to have a uniform edge about 1" tall and even with the edge of the frame rails.

Once the edge is complete, a series of bridle stitches is placed using mattress twine, so that the loops are about 1" tall. Then handfuls of loose horsehair are placed under the bridle stitches to form the first stuffing, after which a thin layer of cotton batting is placed over the horsehair to complete the seat. The cotton batting is not cut; it is gently pulled apart to create a neat edge around all four sides. A "top linen" cover of cotton drill cloth is pinned in place, then folded under to create a neat line along the top of the edge roll, and then stitched in place using a simple whip stitch. This completes the foundation, which should be firm and flat.

Adding the show cover and dust panel

The show cover (leather on this chair) is cut oversized, placed on the frame and tacked underneath – only temporarily at this point – along the front edge and about halfway back on each side. The back of the show cover is then folded back on itself so its leading edge just "kisses" the back legs, where it is marked for a Y-cut that creates three folds: a small triangle at the front, and a long edge fold on either side of the leg. The outside of the leg will require one more cut to remove excess material before it can be neatly folded and tucked in.

Now, working from the centers to the corners, the leather cover is pulled and tacked on the sides of the

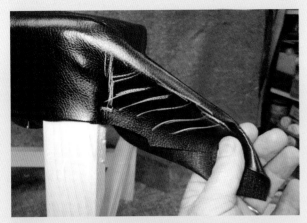

Marking the show cover to remove excess material.

Jute webbing is a modern alternative.

In the more modern approach, the edge roll is more jute webbing, filled with manila rope.

The completed jute edge roll, after tacking.

seat frame so that it is uniform and neat, leaving the front corners until last.

To complete the front corners, the leather from the sides is pulled toward the front and tacked with a "hidden" tack on the front face of the leg. Then the fold of the remaining material can be held out and marked to be cut slightly under the edge of the fold on the inside and then vertically into the corner to remove a triangle of material. The corner is then folded in and temporarily tacked to show the location of the final cut that will create a small triangular fold that will tuck in along the front of the leg. The leather is then tacked and trimmed on the bottom of the seat rails.

A bottom dust cover is optional in traditional work, as it is not clear that they were always installed. A simple black cotton material or "cambric" can be used, and neatly hand-tacked with #3 or #4 tacks.

Seat upholstery with modern materials

The goal of the modern approach is to use more readily available materials and simpler methods to achieve

Rubberized hair goes inside the edge roll.

a high-quality upholstered seat. If done properly the modern version provides a very close approximation of the "sit" and feel of the traditional treatment, while being much less costly and time-consuming. However, the sit of the traditional treatment can vary more widely depending on the amount of loose hair and cotton used.

Cotton batting, attached loosely and hand-pulled to create a neat edge.

A muslin sub-cover is simply tacked on to complete the modern foundation.

On the chair back, the decking is hand-tacked hessian or burlap fabric. Note that this wood chair mockup is different than the project chair, in that the lower section of the crest rail has been completely flattened.

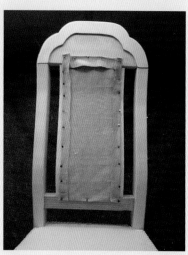

Decorative nails on the chair back.

Replacing the traditional linen webbing in the modern version is standard 3½" red-stripe jute webbing (a black-stripe variety is lighter weight and used only for backrests and arms). The webbing is interwoven, pulled taut with a tined stretcher, and tacked or stapled in place, roughly at the centerline of the tacking rail. A layer of burlap, or canvas duck cloth is cut slightly oversized, then folded back and also tacked near the center of the rail.

The edge roll is created with common ½" manila rope and more jute webbing. Two lengths of rope are joined with loops of electrical tape to form the filling of the edge roll. The webbing is tacked along the outside edge of the frame, folded over to enclose the rope, and then tacked along the inside with #8 tacks.

Once the webbing is tacked on just slightly proud of the edge, a piece of rubberized horsehair is cut to fit snugly in the recess and then covered by a thin layer of upholsterer's cotton or Dacron batting, which does not need to be fastened. The stuffing layers are then covered with a layer of unbleached cotton muslin which is simply pulled neatly and tacked to the sides of the seat rails with #3 or #4 tacks.

The show cover goes on the traditional way.

The chair back is simpler

The treatment of the inside back of this chair is basically the same for both traditional and modern materials. A layer of backing fabric such as hessian or burlap is placed first. The stuffing material for the backrest is just a very thin layer of cotton or Dacron (quilt) batting, and in some early examples there is no stuffing at all. The leather show cover is cut oversized, trimmed neatly and folded under to make a neat edge.

"Nailes" vs. "tacks"

The simple iron fasteners used to hold the under-upholstery materials are called "tacks," and the decorative,

A shop-made nailing guide ensures uniform spacing.

In look and feel, the traditional seat (left) is hard to tell from the version made with more modern materials.

usually brass, rounded-headed ones used for decoration are known as "nailes." It is common to see these chairs referred to traditionally as either "naile'd" or "double naile'd," with the latter indicating that two rows of these expensive shiny fasteners were installed for maximum effect. In either case, a simple shop-made nailing guide will place the nails with uniform 1" spacing.

[1] Coir fiber is the inner strand of the coconut, sometimes called ginger coir for its orange color. Modern "cocomat" doormats and runners are produced from coir. It was widely used as a disposable packing material in the early China trade, and soon adapted as an upholstery stuffing.

[2] Neat is an English term for cows or cattle and is the origin of "neatsfoot oil." Neat leather is cowhide, as opposed to other tanned hides such as goat, which were also used for garments and upholstery.

Suggested reading

James, D. (1999). Upholstery, a complete course. England: Guild of Master Craftsmen.

Graves, L. (2015). Early seating upholstery. Williamsburg, Va.: Colonial Williamsburg Foundation.

Cooke, E. S. (1987). Upholstery in America and Europe from the seventeenth century to World War I. Wayne, Pa.: The Barra Foundation.

Beard, G. (1997). Upholsterers and interior furnishing in England, 1530-1840. New Haven, Conn.: Yale University Press.

Finished mockup of the upholstery for a "crook'd back" chair.

CHAPTER FIVE

Queen Anne Stool c. 1740

Like William & Mary, the Queen Anne style is named for an English monarch. Queen Anne took the throne upon the death of her sister, Queen Mary, in 1702 and ruled until her own death in 1714. In the Colonies there was, to use historian Benno Forman's term, a "provincial lag," making Queen Anne the fashion from 1725 until roughly 1760. British furniture scholars refer to this style of furniture as "early Georgian, referring to Queen Anne's successor, George I. However, in this country we had no fondness for British rulers named George, so Queen Anne's name lived on as a style for far longer than she ruled over England.

The economy of the Colonies was booming during this period. The raw materials and natural abundance of the New World, combined with the mercantilist economic policies of England, led to a strong shipping trade through the major cities of the period, namely Boston and later Philadelphia. Raw materials went out, and finished goods and colonists came in, including skilled tradespeople who brought the latest furniture designs with them.

Hand in glove with the burgeoning wealth was a new-found sense of optimism. No longer were the colonists struggling to meet the basic challenges of life. At least in the cities, British America was becoming a

With Saw, Plane & Chisel

comfortable place to live, and new wealth enabled the citizens to showcase that comfort.

The Queen Anne style embodies the spirit of this period. The pieces climb higher in stature, as seen in the classic Queen Anne high chest of drawers. The curvaceous cabriole leg replaces the turned trumpet leg, and the elegant pad foot replaces the turned ball of the William & Mary period. In short, the pieces become less conservative, both in stature and proportion.

I have chosen two pieces to represent this fertile period in American furnituremaking: a foot stool with cabriole legs and pad feet, c. 1740; and a slant-top desk with bracket feet, c. 1760. These pieces offer an excellent cross-section of the techniques and decorative elements of the Queen Anne style. Cutting cabriole legs and bracket feet without a band saw can be a bit of a trick, but give it a try. No matter how successful you are, you will learn a lot.

Learn to make a classic cabriole

This stool form was popular from the early Queen Anne period all the way into the Federal era, with cosmetic changes only. The cabriole legs, shown here with an early-style trifid foot, also appear with a slipper foot, a Spanish foot and even a carved ball-and-claw. The basic construction is the same regardless, just take care to allow yourself enough length in the leg stock for the type of foot you choose. An option from the even later neoclassical period is to leave out the cabriole leg completely, trading it for a tapered leg with a spade foot.

The most important lesson of this project is to learn to make a cabriole leg by hand. It is a worthwhile and enjoyable skill that will allow you to build a great number of period pieces without resorting to what I like to call "electrickery." The leg is used on everything from fall front desks (usually a small scale cabriole called a "bandy" leg is used for case pieces like that) all the way up to the mighty chest on chest. Replacing the two front legs of our Boston chair with cabrioles will give you a great primer in Queen Anne chair construction.

For some, the cabriole is the stumbling block to a lifetime of handmade period craftsmanship. Try hard, do your best, and recognize that you'll probably have to scrap a leg or two before you get it right.

And last, this piece has a simple seat, which offers a nice first lesson in upholstery, easier than the extensive seat and back upholstery of the previous project. At the end of this chapter, Michael Mascelli shows you how to make a slip seat that is every bit as classic and durable as the stool itself.

Choose your stock carefully

This piece uses a very small amount of walnut so, if you can, spend the money for the most figured wood you can find, especially for the rails. I bought one figured piece of 2"-thick walnut and resawed the four rails from it.

The leg stock should be at least 3" square in the rough. Pieces like this often can be purchased as turning blanks from specialty woodworking stores, or you can simply rip 12/4 stock to size. Either way, be picky about what you choose. Look for rift-sawn stock, meaning the end grain runs from corner to corner. This ensures that each leg will have a pleasing and consistent grain pattern on both show faces, something you will not have if you buy flat-sawn or quarter-sawn wood.

For the rails, the reference surfaces are the outside face and the bottom edge. Plane them flat and square to each other. The inside face can be left in the rough or with rough plane marks, whichever suits your fancy, but aim for an approximate ⅞" thickness for the four rails.

On the legs, the inside faces are your reference surfaces and should be as flat, straight and square to each other as possible. The outside faces of each leg blank require no planing as those faces will be completely changed as you make the cabriole legs. And last, orient the legs in the stool so that the curve of the end grain faces the outside corner (**Photo 1**).

Make sure to orient the grain in your leg blanks this way. This will ensure a pleasing grain pattern at the knee of the cabriole.

2

Laying out a tenon on one of the rails.

3

Once the tenons are cut, scribe the mortise height to accommodate the tenon.

Lay out a cabriole template in ¼"-thick pine or the like, following the measured drawing. It is especially important that the square block at the top of the leg be sized accurately, so take care when laying this section out. This template will be used to lay out the cabriole shape on both reference faces on all four legs, so don't make it out of flimsy paper or cardboard. Thin pine is my preferred material because it's inexpensive, easy to shape with hand tools, and holds up well enough. Cut out the template with your bowsaw and smooth it to the line with rasps, files and sandpaper.

Mark and cut the joinery

Since this is a stool, a piece of furniture that will be viewed from all sides, there is no real front per se, but it makes sense to act as if there were when arranging and marking the parts.

Some people like to use a cabinetmaker's triangle but I prefer to lay out pieces using RF for right front, RR for right rear, etc. I mark them so that the letters appear right side up when viewed from the front side. Mark the top end grain of your leg blanks with the proper letter combination. On walnut, a dark wood which makes pencil difficult to see, I use either sidewalk chalk or a white compressed artist's charcoal. I also draw an arrow pointing to the outside corner of the leg.

Next, choose the locations for each of your four rails, mark their locations on their inside faces, and crosscut them to rough length. Save all of your offcuts: The leg offcuts will become knee blocks with similar grain and color, and you can make pegs out of the rail offcuts.

Now you can cut the rails to final length and cut the mortise-and-tenon joinery that attaches the rails to the legs. In this case, I cut tenons first. The tenons are ⅜" thick and set back from the outside face of the rail approximately ⅜" (**Photo 2**). Once the tenons fit

well in their mortises, plane the top edges of the rails so they are flush with the tops of the legs. This area will see some decorative work later on, so take your time to make straight and square edges (**Photo 3**).

Cabriole legs start with a top block

The top of a cabriole leg is different from a normal leg, in that it is cut narrower than the bottom section, to let the knee of the cabriole shape flare outward. The square upper section is called the top block, and it is cut flush with the rails, but only as low as their bottom edge. To form it, we need to cut big notches on the outside faces of the legs.

These leg cuts will be about 2" from the back reference faces. To dial in that location precisely, assemble the legs and rails before setting your marking gauge, making sure to leave about ¹⁄₁₆" extra to be planed flush later. Mark the cuts on the top of the legs and carry them onto the faces (**Photo 4**).

4

Testing the fit of the mortise-and-tenon joinery.

5

Scribe the top block from the two reference faces. To help prevent errors, I mark the outside corners.

6

Cut the shoulders for the top block using a crosscut backsaw.

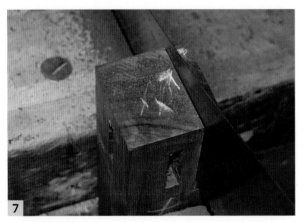

7

Remove the waste using a sharp ripsaw. Stay about ¹⁄₁₆" away from the line, giving you a little waste to pare to ensure the leg and the apron end up flush.

8

A small bit of waste left to clean up with a sharp chisel.

To mark the bottom shoulders of these notches, draw a line that extends from the bottom of each rail across each leg. These are the first cuts to make (**Photos 5-6**). Be very careful not to saw past the layout line that defines the 2"-square block; any stray saw cuts here will be very noticeable and require quite a bit of work to remove.

Once you have the shoulder cuts done, you can saw the waste close to the line (**Photo 7**). Now insert the rails into the legs again, and use the outside rail face to guide a paring chisel as you smooth the outside faces of the legs flush with the rails (**Photos 8-9**).

9

Smooth and ready to proceed.

Place the cabriole template on the outer faces of each leg. The back of the template should be aligned with the interior corner of the leg (top left here), which is the corner made by the two reference faces.

11

The cabriole leg laid out.

12

Draw a straight line that approximates the curved portion of the foot, and pare a small shoulder to give your saw a place to start.

13

The first rip cut.

Rough out the leg with rip cuts

Now you are ready to lay out the cabriole legs. Place the template on one of your reference faces with the rear of the template flush with the back corner (**Photo 10**). Trace around the template with a pencil or white charcoal, whichever you prefer. Remove the template and flip the blank 90° so that the other reference face is up, flip the template over, and align the same template edge with the reference corner. Again, trace around the template (**Photo 11**).

When making cabriole legs, I like to do each step on all four legs before proceeding to the next. This helps to ensure that the legs have a similar character at the end. However, there will be some variation no matter what

you do. This is something that should be celebrated as a mark of hand work rather than denigrated as a flaw.

In most modern furniture shops a cabriole leg would be sawed out with a band saw. Since we are pretending that band saws haven't yet been invented, we'll do the majority of the stock removal with a traditional ripsaw, just as it might have been done 200 years ago. Draw an angled line that starts near the transition point between the foot area and the ankle, comes within ¼" or so of the knee outline, and extends to the outside face of the leg (**Photo 12**). Then draw a line that connects that low transition point to the toes of the foot (**Photo 13**). Do this on both reference faces of all four legs. Next, use your ripsaw and saw these lines on both faces. (**Photos 14-15**).

14

Make a longer rip cut from the knee to the end of the first rip cut, forming the leg and foot.

15

Repeat the cuts on the opposite face to finish roughing in the leg blank.

16

With the four legs roughed in and the stool dry-assembled, you can get a sense of its appearance.

Next, to get ready for roughing out the rear curve, saw stopping cuts into both reference faces. Make this cut at the deepest point of the curve (**Photo 17**). Then, using a chisel bevel down and working from the top of the leg down, pare a curve into both faces that follows the pencil line (**Photos 18-20**). This should be done evenly on both sides or the leg will look lopsided, but if you make a small mistake here it can be evened out during the rest of the process.

To work from the bottom of the leg up, along the shallower curve, I like to use a drawknife, which removes wood more quickly while producing a smoother curve. But the chisel technique would also work.

Curved guide lines define the contours

When you finish with the drawknife, you have completed the rough work on the leg. Every corner of the leg must now be rounded off to some extent, beginning with the ankle and foot transition. To guide your work, you need a new series of layout lines.

Take your white charcoal and mark a center line on each face at the ankle. On the two front faces, continue the line up the leg toward the knee, keeping the line at about the same distance from the front corner. Draw another line up from the ankle to the knee, this time parallel with the back of the leg and set in from it roughly half the ankle thickness. Now, draw a line halfway between one of the edges and the closest par-

17

Two stopping cuts let you use a chisel and drawknife to rough out the back curves.

18

Chop out the upper curve with a chisel, used bevel down.

19

Detail of the chisel work. The ridges will be removed during leg-shaping process.

20

Make sure the curve is smooth and follows your layout line closely. I carve out the lower curve with a drawknife.

21

The white charcoal guide lines. Once you make it this far, clear your mind and proceed carefully, or you will make a beautiful piece of firewood.

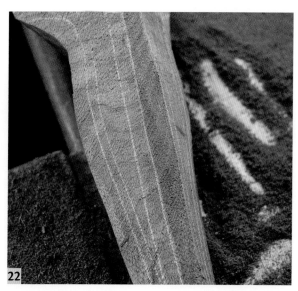

22

The front corners, beveled to the guide lines with a cabinetmaker's rasp. The rear corners are next.

allel line. Repeat this step for the other line. If you do this properly, each face of the leg should have four lines drawn on it (**Photo 21**).

To hold the leg firmly and conveniently for shaping, clamp it lengthwise in a pipe clamp and secure the clamp in your face vise. Using a cabinetmaker's rasp, bevel off all four corners on each leg, using the outermost lines as your guide (**Photo 22**). As you work, make sure you keep the bevels even along their length. Once you have the bevels done, switch to a fine rasp and smooth the corners left by the previous step, working to the innermost lines on each leg face (**Photo 23**). Make each corner of the leg a smooth radius without facets, switching to a mill file (and scrapers if necessary) to get the final smoothness (**Photo 24**). Finally, use the round side of the file to smooth the area where the leg curves into the foot, also known as the ankle.

Finish with the feet

The early-Queen Anne original this stool is based on had a rather crude version of the classic trifid foot. Keeping with the spirit of the original, I chose to replicate the feet exactly. A later trifid can be done if you so choose. *Popular Woodworking Magazine* had a nice article on that topic in the August 2012 issue.

To begin, saw each leg to its final length per the measured drawing. This will leave you with a roughly square block at the bottom of the leg. Make a template per the drawing and place it on the bottom of the leg so that the flat edges of the template align with the two inner reference faces (**Photo 25**). Trace around

23

To round the bevels you just made, work to the next set of layout lines with a fine rasp. Ideally, this will result in a round profile.

24

Except for some minor tool marks, the legs are done and I'm ready to carve the feet.

25 Place the trifid foot pattern on the leg blank and mark the bottom of the feet.

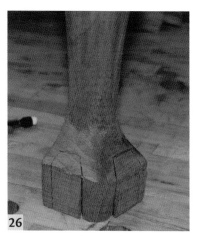

26 The foot trimmed up and ready to carve. The lines were carried up from the bottom of the feet.

27 Backsaw cuts define the toes. Take care not to saw too deeply.

28 Use an in-cannel gouge to mark and cut the round shapes between the toes.

29 Round off and undercut the toes using an out-cannel gouge. Smooth the ankle transition to complete the foot.

the template with a pencil, carry the toe lines onto the front of the feet, and then saw the outside edges of the large central toe, as well as the inside of the two flanking toes (**Photos 26-27**).

Working to those saw cuts, use an in-cannel gouge (I used a ½" firmer gouge) to mark and remove the waste between the toes (**Photo 28**). The area between the toes will automatically take the shape of the gouge, giving you a consistent size and shape for all the feet. Next, using an out-cannel gouge (a No. 5 sweep, ⅝" carver's gouge, in this case), round off each toe, under-

cutting them so the foot is smaller at the bottom than it is at the top (**Photo 29**). Last, smooth up the foot with your rasp, a scraper and sandpaper, paying special attention to the ankle to ensure a smooth transition from the leg to the foot.

Rabbet and mould the rails

This stool will have a slip seat, meaning a separate seat frame that slides into the stool and is housed in a rabbet. To lay out the seat rabbet, scribe a line along the top edge, ⅜" from the front face, and then scribe

Lay out the rails for the seat and moulding rabbets.

30

31

The moving fillister cuts the outside rabbet and the sash fillister cuts the seat rabbet.

32

Carrying the seat rabbet into the legs. You can see the telltale marks of the auger I used to waste away the inside corner.

another line 2½" up from the bottom reference edge. At the same time, lay out the rabbet on the outside edge that will help to form the moulding there (**Photo 30**). It is ⅜" wide by ⅛" deep. You can cut the rabbets however you like. I use the moving fillister for the outside rabbet and my sash fillister for the seat rabbet (**Photo 31**).

Continuing the seat rabbet onto the tops of the legs is a little more difficult. I start by drilling a relief hole with a brace and center bit at the inside corner of the rabbet on each leg. Then I saw horizontally, on a diagonal, across the inside corner to free as much waste as possible. From there it is easy to chop out the bulk of the waste with a chisel, and finish down to the lines with finer cuts (**Photo 32**).

The small thumbnail moulding also continues from the rails onto the tops of the legs. To do this, I dry-fit the legs and rails and carry the rabbet location onto the legs. Then I use my moving fillister to continue the rabbets across the leg grain (**Photo 33**).

Begin the thumbnail moulding on the legs by cutting a rabbet.

33

With that done, I grab a No. 6 hollow moulding plane and round over the corner on both the rails and the legs, taking great care on the latter (**Photo 34**). If the iron is sharp and set to take a shallow cut, you will be able to cut the moulding across the grain. If it tears, simply grab a file and complete the work. At assembly, you will smooth over the intersections between the rails and legs, so it is better to leave a little extra wood here at this point.

Cut the lower rail curves

The final step before gluing the stool together is to cut the scrollwork on the seat rails. A flat should be left on each end of each rail, as this is where the knee blocks will ultimately attach. The shorter rail gets a simple profile, while the longer rail has a serpentine pattern. Both begin 2" from the shoulders, leaving a flat area where the knee blocks are attached (see below).

Using the pattern provided, make a template for the long-rail pattern. Draw the profile on each rail, cut it out using your bowsaw, and smooth down to the line with a rasp and sandpaper (**Photos 35-41**).

For the short rails, no pattern is necessary. Simply draw a line ¾" from the bottom edge, connecting it to perpendicular lines that start 2" from each shoulder. Now use a French curve or any round object to turn those square corners into round ones. Cut with your bowsaw and smooth to the line with rasps and sandpaper.

34

Roughly round off the leg moulding. The final fairing of this rounded edge should be done after assembly.

35

Use a template to lay out the scrollwork on the long rails.

36

Begin by cutting the central fillets with a crosscut backsaw.

37

Knock out the waste with a sharp chisel.

38

Cut close to the curve with a bowsaw. Stay on the waste side of the line.

39

After being sawn, the curves will be smoothed with a rasp and sandpaper.

40

One apron cut and ready for smoothing.

41

Bevel the inside edges with the rasp. Also visible here is the rough-sawn surface on the interior of the rails, left over from the resawing process. Smooth it up if you like.

42

The shorter side aprons have a simplified profile.

Dry-assemble your piece one final time, adjust the fit of any recalcitrant joinery, and be sure that the frame is square. Now take the piece apart for the final time and prepare for the glue up.

Assemble in stages

I like to glue the two side assemblies together before adding the front and rear rails and finishing the job. This makes the glue-up less hectic. Once the glue is dry but before you remove the clamps, bore two ¼" dia. holes through each mortise-and-tenon joint, and make pegs from the rail offcuts you saved.

To make the pegs, start with square pieces and just roughly round them with a chisel. Sharpen the end a little before applying glue and driving them home with a mallet. Take care to make your pegs from straight grained stock and make sure to drive them straight, as an angled blow can fracture the peg before it is all the way home. It's also possible to break off the peg below the surface of the joint, forcing you to bore it out after it dries and start over.

If you don't want to make pegs, ¼" walnut dowel stock is available at most home improvement and wood-working stores; just be sure that the dowel diameter matches the diameter of your peg holes (store-bought dowels tend to run small so be careful).

When the glue is dry, saw off the pegs close to the joint surface and pare them flush with a sharp chisel.

Add the knee blocks

Part of what makes a cabriole leg so elegant are the small knee blocks that ease its transition into the rails. When the assembly is dry and pegged, it is time to make and attach those rounded blocks. They are an important part of the overall design and care needs to be taken to get them right.

Start with the offcuts you removed from the leg blanks. In a piece like this, the grain of the knees should run vertically to match the grain in the legs themselves. Saw the offcuts apart on a diagonal line (**Photo 43**).

Find one of the reference faces that you planed smooth and square and hold that face up to the inside face of the right front leg, with the end of the block flush against the bottom of the seat rail. Then use a pencil to trace the outside surface of the leg's knee onto the side of the knee block, transferring the shape. With that finished, remove most of the waste on the front face of the block with backsaw and chisel cuts before rounding it off close to the line with a rasp. Glue and nail the block in place and allow it to dry before continuing (**Photos 44-45**). Repeat these steps for all eight knee blocks.

When the glue is dry, you can refine the shape of the knee blocks. Since the heavy shaping is already done, you only have to remove a small amount of wood to get the blocks and legs to flow together smoothly. I like to

43

Cut the knee blocks from the leg offcuts. For a good color and grain match, keep the offcuts together with the leg they were sawed from.

44

Glue the blocks in place and then finish shaping the curve, bringing it flush with the leg along its front face and bottom edge.

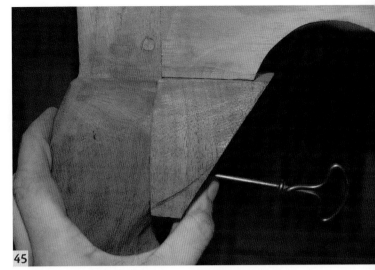

45

Using a gimlet to predrill for a nail. This will hold the knee block in place while the glue dries. Drive it extra deep so it doesn't interfere with final shaping.

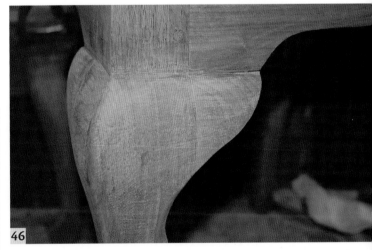

46

The knee block smoothed and ready to finish.

use a paring chisel (as deadly sharp as I know how to make it) diagonally across the grain to smooth the glue line between the block and the leg. When the bulk of the material is removed, you can scrape or sand smooth the outside of the block. The bottom edge of the knee block also requires some final shaping and fairing to complete the smooth convex curve that connects the leg to the bottom of the rails. Watch out for the nail in this area. Most of the work is done with a rasp and guided by eye, but you can make a template if you don't feel confident. However you choose to proceed, make the bottom curve smooth to the eye and hand.

Finishing options

Cabriole legs are notoriously difficult to finish evenly because there is a fair amount of end grain exposed along the sinuous curves. End grain soaks up more oil and stain than long-grain areas do, which can make the finish look blotchy. The original had this mottled coloring, perhaps to a greater extent than some would like to see.

I chose to replicate the original finish, applying a light coat of linseed oil to the piece before applying four coats of blonde shellac, and then rubbing out the shellac with a dark brown paste wax and 0000 steel wool. This gave my piece the color variation you see here, both within the legs themselves and between the legs and the rails.

If you would rather achieve a more uniform color, try applying a thin "spit coat" of blonde shellac – somewhere in the neighborhood of a ½-lb. cut – to seal the grain – before applying any oil or stain to darken the piece overall.

If you mess up the finish entirely, you can always paint it with milk paint. But for your own sanity (and the sake of the beautiful walnut you used), please try the natural finish. Can you tell I have a soft spot for walnut?

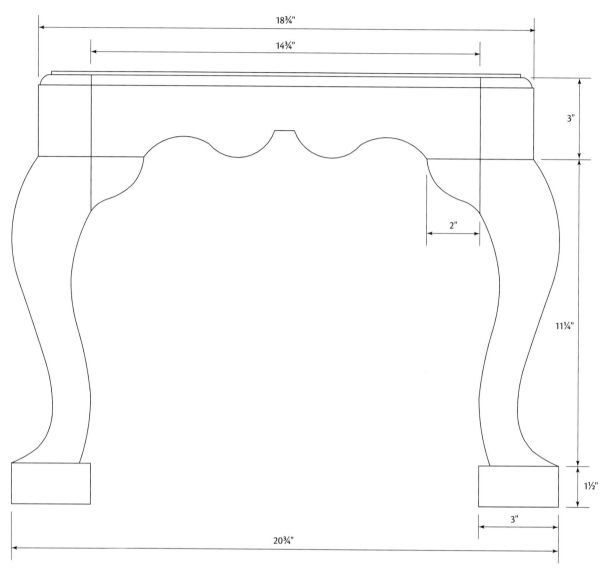

ELEVATION

QUEEN ANNE STOOL
OVERALL DIMENSIONS: 16⅜" DEEP X 20¾" WIDE X 15¾" TALL

Qty	Part	Dimensions (inches)			stock	comment
		Thickness	Width	Length		
4	Cabriole legs	3	3	15¾	walnut	
8	Knee blocks	2	3	3	walnut	Blank dimension
2	Short seat rails	¾	3	11⅞	walnut	¾" tenon on both ends
2	Long seat rails	¾	3	16¼	walnut	¾" tenon on both ends
2	Short slip seat sides	¾	1½	11⅞	walnut	¾" tenon on both ends
2	Long slip seat sides	¾	1½	17¾	walnut	

Notes: Rough cut all parts oversize then cut to fit.

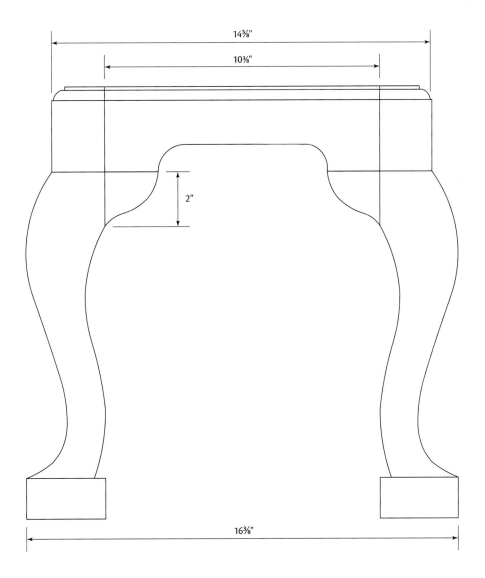

14⅜"

10⅜"

2"

16⅜"

PROFILE

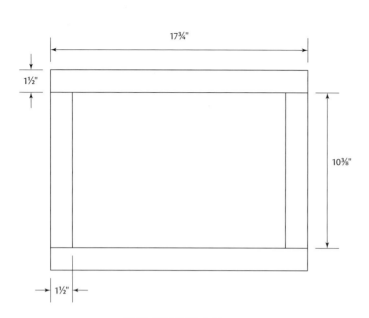

SLIP SEAT PLAN

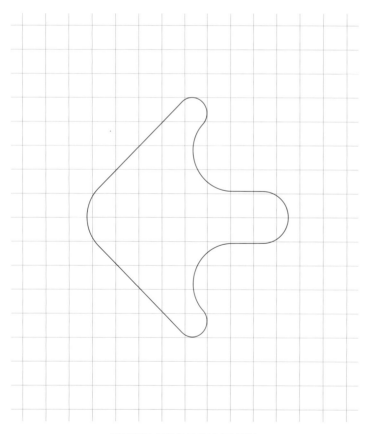

TRIFID FOOT PATTERN
One square = ⅛"

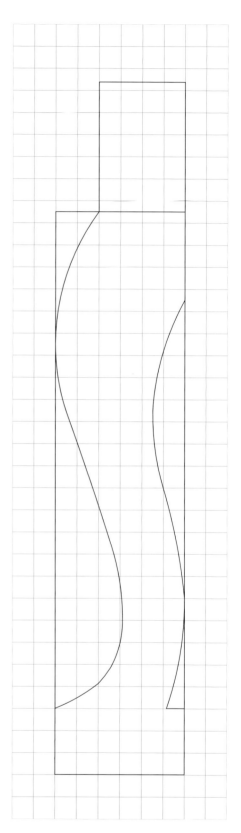

CABRIOLE LEG PATTERN
One square = ½"

Upholstering a Simple Slip Seat

By Michael Mascelli

The evolution of chair design was not so much a continuum as it was a few brilliant outbursts of design creativity, combined with an equal degree of panic on the part of the workers charged with executing the increasingly challenging designs.

One of the most creative periods was the turn of the 18th century, when chairs were finally freed from older, boxy, utilitarian forms to take on lighter, far more elegant lines in legs, backs and upholstered elements. Leaving behind the heavy upholstery that relied on big fasteners driven into sturdy tacking rails, many designers adopted a removable or "slip" seat frame that could be upholstered as a separate unit and simply dropped into a recess created by a rabbet in the frame rails.

In the earliest forms, such as this Queen Anne stool, slip seat frames were simply well-joined and then beveled around the outside edge to create a slightly raised field in the middle. For these pieces the emphasis was on the chair – often the design of the back splat – and the seat was simply a necessary feature whose purpose was to support the sitter and not detract from the overall design. So these early slip seats are plain, very lightly padded, and only slightly more comfortable than sitting on a solid piece of wood.

The process

The seat foundation is 2" black-and-white linen webbing, which is installed on top of the frame with a toggle-type strainer, in a simple 2-by-3 woven pattern. The webbing is pulled taut, but not so much that it distorts the shape of the frame, which is surprisingly easy to do.

It is important to insure that the webbing is tacked on the flat middle part of the frame, not on the beveled edges, and that the webbing tacks are not all in a straight line, which could split the frame.

A piece of sturdy hessian, burlap or canvas forms the deck. It is neatly folded under and tacked on a line just outside the webbing tacks, using #6 tacks this time.

Next a thin layer of loose horsehair is placed on top of the decking – kept inside the border by about 1" all around. Use a regulator (thick, needle-like upholstery

A toggle-type strainer pulls the webbing taut for tacking.

The completed black-and-white linen webbing.

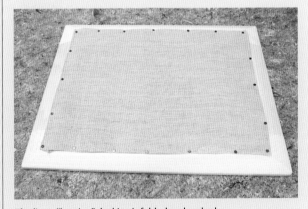

The linen "hessian" decking is folded and tacked.

A thin layer of loose horsehair goes in the middle.

Cotton batting comes next, regulated to form a tapered edge.

Pull the muslin sub-cover tight and tack it to the bottom of the frame.

The show cover is also pulled tight, and then tacked everywhere but the corners.

tool) to achieve even distribution and uniform density of the horsehair, as it will be held in place only by the layers that come next. Now add a thin layer of cotton batting, which will require splitting the batting in thickness, or just use thinner Dacron batting. It is important to regulate or "tease" the cotton along the edges to form a shape that follows the profile of the beveled edges of the frame underneath.

A layer of unbleached muslin or light cotton fabric provides the sub-cover, which holds the horsehair and cotton in place. Working from the center to the corners on each side, pull and tack the muslin to the bottom of the frame using #4 tacks.

The leather show cover is tacked to the bottom of the frame along the center of these rails only, leaving the corners untacked. That lets you fold and mark the corners, and remove the excess. Do that and then complete the tacking. A plain black cotton or cambric dust cover can be added to the bottom if desired.

Fold the corners to mark and cut away the excess.

The completed slip seat.

Finished slip seat showing tapered sides and flat loft.

CHAPTER SIX

Queen Anne Desk c. 1760

With its upper compartment, drop lid and banks of lipped drawers, this classic desk is the most ambitious project in the book. But if you complete it, you'll have the ability to build just about any dovetailed case in the 18th century.

This desk design is also highly adaptable. It can be modified to represent a slightly earlier time period by simply changing the feet from bracket to ball. You could choose to inlay a compass rose into the outside face of the desk lid, which would make it similar to Boston pieces of the period. And if you need a chest of drawers more than a desk, you can omit the angled sides, extend the top the full depth of the case, and just add more dividers and drawers.

Start with the sides

Like the original, this piece is made from figured maple. To begin, glue up the boards for the case sides, top and bottom, and mill them to size and thickness. The boards for the case top and sides should be the most attractive boards you can find. The reference edge on the sides, bottom and top is the front edge. The reference face is the inside of the case; that's where the joinery happens and thus where flatness matters most.

Once you have the sides cut to size, use a marking gauge to lay out the ⅜"-by-⅜" rabbets for the back boards, but don't cut them yet. First cut the dados for the drawer dividers and the bottom boards in the desk interior.

Lay out the ⅞"-wide, ⅜"-deep dados for the dividers. This is best done by clamping the sides together and marking the dados on both front edges at the same time (**Photo 1**), and then using a square and knife to carry those lines onto the inside faces. Scribe the ⅜" depth of the dado on those front edges, and then get ready to cut the dados (**Photo 2**). Because the sides are so wide, I used a long fence to guide my saw (**Photos 3-4**). After chiseling out the waste, use a router plane to work down to the depth line (**Photo 5**).

Also cut the long dado for the two interior floor boards. The rear interior board is rabbeted to overlap the front one, but they both fit into the same straight dado because the ends of the rear board are also rabbeted to create a tongue. That does leave space in the dado below the rear board, but that gets filled later with a small strip of wood.

1

Clamp the sides together to lay out the dados for the drawer dividers. This helps to ensure that the case comes out square.

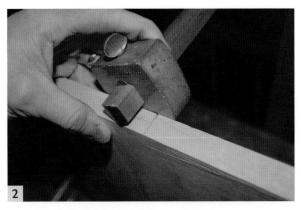

2

Scribe the depth of the dados with a marking gauge. Be sure to run the fence of the gauge on the reference (inside) face.

3

Chisel the layout lines before sawing to prevent chipping across the grain.

4

Use a fence to guide the saw when cutting these long dados.

5

After you remove the waste with a chisel as described in Chapter 3, a router plane cuts the dado to finished depth.

6

The case back rabbet, which will house the pine back boards.

7

A quick check to make sure that the case dados line up with each other.

8

Lay out the drop-front angle while the case boards are still aligned.

9

Crosscut on the waste side of the pencil line and plane the surface smooth, leaving the line. Later, you will trim this surface with a fine-set plane to adjust the fit of the lid.

When the dados are done, cut the rabbets for the back boards with either a moving fillister or a square rabbet plane (**Photo 6**). By doing this after cutting the dados, you will clean up any damage that might occur where the router plane exits the back edges.

Cut matching angles for the drop front

After cutting the dados, you need to lay out and cut the angled edges that the drop front will rest on when the desk is closed. It is best to cut both of these angles simultaneously to ensure that both sides will be exactly the same.

Use the dados to line up the sides as you clamp their inside faces tightly together (**Photo 7**). Lay out the angle on one side's show face and then carry the lines over to the other side's show face using a square (**Photo 8**). Connect the lines with a straightedge and a pencil, and then scribe your pencil lines with a knife. This will prevent the crosscut saw from taking extra chunks out of the grain on these long angled crosscuts.

Take care to keep your cut square and about $\frac{1}{16}$" off the waste side of the line. Then plane the sawn surface so it is square across both case sides, and perfectly aligned, before unclamping the sides (**Photo 9**). This step is arguably the most important for the successful fit and finish of the drop front. If the angles are not aligned, the desk will not close properly.

Dovetail the case bottom

With the sides done, you can dovetail the case together. The case bottom is attached with through dovetails. The tails should be on the bottom board (**Photo 10**). Take your time and make joints that will hold the parts together, but don't spend a lot of time making them perfect. The joints are hidden from every angle, so look at this as an opportunity to practice making quick yet functional dovetails.

If you prepared your stock by hand, it is unlikely that your case bottom is exactly consistent in thickness. You'll have to take this variation into account, so, instead of using a marking gauge to scribe the dovetail baselines, use the board itself to scribe its thickness onto its mate (**Photos 11-12**). With this exception, follow the techniques described in Chapter 2 to join the case bottom. (**Photos 13-16**).

10

11

12

The case bottom. Knots are okay, as are chunky, ugly dovetails. Speed is the name of the game.

Clamp the boards together to scribe their baselines. Handplaned boards are rarely consistent in thickness, so direct scribing, from one board to the other, is better than using a marking gauge.

13

Sawing the case-bottom dovetails.

14

Chopping out the waste.

15 Preparing to cut the pins on the case side.

16 Checking the final fit. Strength matters here, but not looks.

Add the floor boards and dovetail the case top

You are ready to add the top to the case, but there will be a couple of necessary interruptions along the way. The case top is attached with half-blind dovetails, so to determine its true length, which extends from the baseline of the pins on one case side to the baseline on the other side, it helps to make and temporarily install the floor boards that form the interior of the desk opening and dry-clamp the case together.

Dry fit the bottom of the case into the sides, and measure across the bottom to figure out how long the interior floor boards should be, factoring in the depth of their dados. Cut and plane them to length so they fit into the case, with the width of the case being exactly the same at these floor boards as it is at the bottom of the case.

Now is as good a time as any to finish those floor boards. Rabbet and mould the rear board so it interlocks with the front one (**Photo 17**). Since the rear board sits higher and is rabbeted at its ends to create a narrow tongue, you'll also need small blocks to fill the back of the dados below the tongue.

Return to the dovetailing process. Dry-clamp the case, with the case bottom and floor boards in place, and use a marking gauge to scribe the pin baseline along the top of each case side, ⅝" from the inside reference face. Now you can place the top onto the sides, and transfer those pin baselines to the top board, marking its ultimate length (**Photo 18**).

The added difficulty here is that the front edge of the top will be planed flush with the angled front edge

17 The interior floor boards interlock, and a decorative moulding softens the edge.

18 Scribing the length of the top board.

of the case sides. So before unclamping the case and moving the top, scribe its width also, making sure to add an extra inch or so in width to account for the beveled area along the front edge (**Photo 19**).

Saw the top board to the length and width you marked out. Make sure to place the extra width at the front as you cut the ⅜"-by-⅜" rabbet on the back edge to house the back boards (**Photo 20**).

Now you can cut the dovetails on the top of the case, but not the mating pins just yet. Lay out and cut the tails using the same ⅝" marking gauge setting you used on the case sides. Make sure that you don't place a tail in the extra width you left at the front edge of the top (**Photo 21**). In that area, you will simply leave a longer shoulder. Take great care to make a square, clean cut in this spot as this joint will be extremely visible and any flaws will ruin the look of the project (**Photo 22**).

Extra width on the board will allow you to saw and plane the case angle on the top.

Make sure to rabbet the top for the back boards.

Laying out the dovetails in the top of the case.

The extra width will be planed off at the case angle.

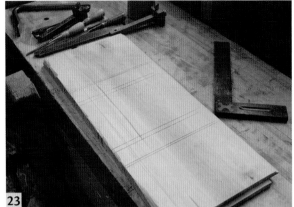

Line up the case top and the rear floor board to mark the dados that will house the interior dividers. **23**

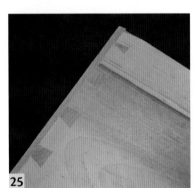

24

Scribe the dovetails onto the case sides. A pencil will work, but a knife is better.

The finished dovetails. **25**

26

Scribe the case angle onto the top board.

Take a moment to dado the parts for the vertical dividers

Next, install the rear board and run a pencil line on it where the case sides and the rear board intersect. This line will allow you to align the rear interior board with the case top so that you can mark the interior dados for the vertical dividers in the desk interior (**Photo 23**). Cut the dados, and then plane the edge moulding on the interior rear board.

Re-assemble and re-clamp the case, and use the tail board to scribe the pins onto the case sides (**Photo 24**). Now you can cut the pins. Check the fit of the dovetails and make adjustments as necessary. Focus on achieving a good tight fit on the top show surface as this is an important cosmetic area (**Photo 25**).

Bevel the top edge and glue up the case

The final step before gluing up the case is beveling the front of the top flush with the slanted case sides. Scribe the angles from the case sides onto the extra width left on the top board (**Photo 26**). Remove the board from the case sides, clamp it to your benchtop, saw close to the line with a ripsaw and clean up the cut with your jointer plane (**Photo 27**). With that done, flip the board

27

The bevel after rip-sawing and planing.

on edge and plane off the sharp point so that it makes a square corner with the case's angled face (**Photo 28**).

Finally, put the final smooth surface on the case sides, top and interior floor boards with your smoothing plane. With these steps done, go ahead and glue the case together. Glue in the rear floor board as well, but leave the front floor board out.

Install the drawer dividers

The drop front of this desk is supported on two thin pieces of wood called lopers. Those are pulled out of the case before the top is opened and slid back in after the top is closed. The lopers require vertical side supports to be dadoed into the interior front board and the first drawer divider to control their movement (**Photo 29**).

Start by making the drawer dividers to fit the case. Then, with the front interior board and the first divider in place without glue, lay out the loper-support dados on the top of the first divider and the bottom of the front interior board. The dados are ⅞" wide and ⅜" deep, located ⅞" from the interior faces of the case sides.

Feel free to saw past the termination point for the dado on the bottom of the front interior board, as the original reflects this time-saving action (**Photo 30**). Remove most of the waste with a chisel and finish to the depth line with the router plane (**Photo 31**).

Now you can apply glue and slide in in the front interior board and the first divider, and then glue in

28

Plane the top to match the angle of the sides, and then plane a bevel below that edge, to receive the desk lid squarely.

29

The drawer lopers support the desk lid. They should have a somewhat loose fit in the openings to ensure that they will always open smoothly, even in humid conditions.

30

The housing for the loper divider requires two saw cuts and chisel work. The chisel work is easier if you overcut the sides (as done on the original).

31

The completed housing. A bit of roughness on the bottom isn't a problem.

32

The case glue up can be nerve-wracking. Take your time and use plenty of clamps.

33

Drawer runners go in next, glued only near the front of their dados. Fast-setting hot hide glue will let you rub the runners into place without clamps.

34

The glue block in place. Notice that it sticks down below the foot about ⅛", meaning that the desk rests on the block and not on the decorative feet.

35

Planing the straight grained stock for the base.

the loper supports in as well (**Photo 32**). Then its time to cut, fit and glue in the drawer runners (**Photo 33**). Make sure to apply glue only to the front half of the dado; if you glue the full length of the runners, they will try to stop the case sides from moving seasonally, and probably cause them to crack. It will be very difficult to get clamps on these runners, especially near the front of the case, so I recommend that you rub them into place with a fast-setting adhesive like hot hide glue.

Making the mitered bracket base

With the case basically done, it is time to make the base that it sits on. Although the desk appears to sit on its bracket feet, it actually rests on interior glue blocks

that protrude about ⅛" below each foot (**Photo 34**). The blocks help to hold the mitered corners of the feet together, and also take the punishment when the desk is dragged around. Most importantly, they carry the weight of the desk, letting the bracket base be mostly decorative.

To make the bracket base, choose a piece of maple that is as straight grained as possible, and long enough to wrap around the case with at least 6" extra for trimming and fitting (**Photo 35**). This will help ensure that the moulding process goes smoothly. Following the hand-tool moulding practices described in Chapter 3, plane the blank to the required profile (**Photo 36**).

36

The top edge of the base should be moulded before the blank is cut into mitered sections.

37

Center the base blank on the front of the case and scribe the case width onto the blank to prepare for mitering.

Flip the case onto its back, leaving the bottom end of the case sticking out over the edge of the bench. Mark the center of both the blank and the front of the case, and lay the moulding on the case with those marks aligned (**Photo 37**). Now you can run a pencil on the back of the moulding where touches the outside of each case side. This line represents the inside edge of the miter you have to cut at each front corner. Cut your miters, leaving about ⅟₁₆" of wood beyond the line for final fitting. Cut the complimentary miters on each of the remaining two pieces but leave the other ends long, as this gives you a margin for error should you have to trim more off the miter to get a good fit.

Clamp those side pieces onto the case in order to mark the cuts at their back ends and also fit the front base piece exactly (**Photo 38**).

At this time, you should also make the pine baseboard for the rear. This is not moulded and simply butts into the interior face of the side mouldings (**Photo 39**). The top edge of this board will eventually be glued to the bottom board of the case.

With the miters cut and fit, it is time to define the shape of the feet. Cut the same profile on both ends of each piece; I like to use a coping saw to do this. Smooth the cuts with files, slightly back-beveling the curved face so that it doesn't visually intrude into the negative space.

Now you can attach the mitered and shaped base pieces to the case with glue and brads, ensuring that the top edges of the mouldings completely cover up the side case dovetails. With the mouldings in place, trim the rear baseboard to final length and glue it into place.

Prepare glue blocks that are small enough to be concealed within the bottom of the bracket foot. I

38

Clamp the extra-long side pieces onto the case to fit the front piece.

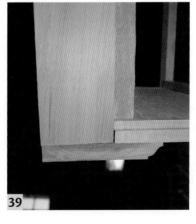

39

The rear base board simply butts into the side base pieces and is glued along the top edge onto the bottom board. Glue blocks further support this piece.

A sample glue block. The beveled corner fits into the joint and helps ensure a good glue bond in case the joint is less than square. The bottom of the foot (top in the picture) should be chamfered on all edges to prevent splitting.

40

41

The glue block in place. Notice that it sticks down below the foot about ⅛", meaning that the desk rests on the block and not on the decorative feet.

42

Rabbet the top edge and ends of the inset drawer fronts.

43

Add the rabbet for the drawer bottom. This will be hidden by a half-tail on the drawer side.

tend to use pine, with the bottom corners knocked off (**Photo 40**). The interior edges – those that will be hidden within the corner of the feet – should also be beveled off.

Glue the blocks to the each side of the interior corner of the base moulding, positioned so that the top of each block butts into the case bottom. Once the glue has dried, trim the blocks to stick out ⅛" lower than the bottom of each foot (**Photo 41**).

Rabbeted drawers are trickier

The drawer fronts are rabbeted to overlap the case and the drawer dividers by about ⅜" on each end and along the top edge. This adds some difficulty but really makes for a nice looking piece. The process for lipped drawers starts with measuring the drawer openings, adding ¾" to the width and ⅜" to the height, and then preparing the drawer-front stock to those sizes. Next cut a rabbet on each end and along the top edge of each drawer front (**Photo 42**). Test and adjust the fit of each front in its drawer opening, and then rabbet the lower inside edge for the drawer bottom (**Photo 43**).

Next, prepare the stock for your drawer sides and backs to the width of the rabbeted section of the drawer front and cut a ¼"-wide by ⅜"-deep. rabbet in each part to house the drawer bottoms (**Photo 44**). After you

44

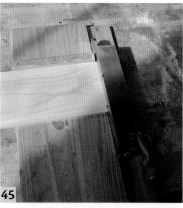
45

If you are careful with your backsaw, you may not need to shoot the ends of the drawer parts. I obviously wasn't careful enough.

Rabbeting the drawer sides prior to crosscutting them to length.

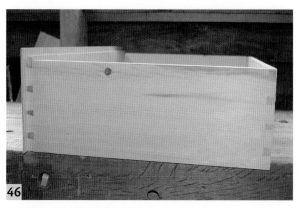
46

The completed drawer joint.

47

A few over-cuts never hurt anyone.

have this rabbet cut, you can crosscut the drawer pieces to length. I use a shooting board on these crosscuts to make sure they are as accurate as possible (**Photo 45**).

Each drawer has half-blind dovetails at the front and through-dovetails at the back (**Photo 46**). I like to lay out my dovetails by eye as I prefer a little variance, but feel free to lay them out as carefully as you like.

Cut your dovetails using the techniques in Chapter 2, but focus on achieving a tight, attractive joint for the half-blinds at the front. When cutting the pins, you'll have more chiseling to do than normal. You can over-cut into the inside face of the drawer, as usual, but you won't be able to saw down as far as normal without cutting into the overhanging lip (**Photo 47**). If you cut into that outer lip it will look terrible. "Flawed" period construction techniques notwithstanding, I have never seen a stray saw cut on an overlapped drawer front.

Once you have the drawers dovetailed and glued together, plane or scrape the thumbnail moulding on the front face of the drawer fronts (**Photo 48**). Then cut, fit and nail in your drawer bottoms and drawer slips. Finally, test the fit of the drawers and adjust as necessary to make a smoothly operating drawer.

Fit the desk interior

Prepare the vertical drawer divider stock to rough size and then shoot the ends to fit the pieces precisely into their dados. Once you have a good fit, mark the location of the horizontal drawer divider boards on the vertical dividers and the case sides. I use a story stick to do this, rather than relying on a ruler (**Photo 49**).

Cut the necessary dados in the dividers and case sides using the same saw-and-chisel method you used to cut the other interior dados, and then fit the horizontal

48

The drawer fronts get another rabbet on their front edges – and a curved moulding.

49

Use a story stick to lay out the interior drawer dividers. This is both quicker and more accurate than measuring.

The interior drawer openings, completed and ready for drawers. **50**

dividers and glue them in place (**Photo 50**). Make sure to take your time on this step to achieve a good fit. Any gaps here will be very noticeable and will make your project look poorly done.

With the openings prepared, cut your interior drawer pieces to size and plane a ¼"-by-¼" rabbet along the bottom edge of each piece. Carefully plane the drawer fronts to fit into the openings you just defined with the drawer dividers (**Photo 51**).

After that, gang-cut the tails on the drawer sides, one pair at a time. This speeds the job and maintains a consistent look. Join the drawer fronts to the sides using half-blind dovetails as you did when you joined the case top to the case sides (**Photo 52**). Make your drawer backs to fit and join them using through dovetails. Cut the drawer bottoms to size and glue them into place. Pre-drill a hole for the pull in the center of each drawer front.

The tall, narrow openings are designed for letter drawers. You could also leave them as open space for tall papers. These drawers are simply rabbeted and nailed. Prepare drawer fronts that fit the openings, and then cut a ¼"-by-¼" rabbet on both sides and along the bottom edge. Now prepare ¼"-thick stock for the sides and ¾" thick pieces for the back. Nail the sides into the rabbets at the front of the drawers and then nail the back in.

Nail the bottom on, then pre-drill a hole for the pull knob. I chose to reed these drawer fronts to simulate columns, using a No. 4 hollow and a No. 4 round plane to mould the reeds into the front, after first dividing area into eight equal portions and carving a starting groove for the hollows with a small gouge (**Photos 53-54**).

Breadboard ends stabilize the lid

Traditionally the lid of the desk served two functions. The first was to allow the owner to close and lock the desk, protecting the interior drawers and their contents from snooping eyes. Then, when folded down

51

The drawer fronts are planed to fit the openings prior to dovetailing. Use the most figured wood you have for these fronts.

52

Like the bigger drawers, the interior drawers have half-blind dovetails at the front, through dovetails in the back, and rabbeted-in drawer bottoms.

53

Laying out the reeding for the letter drawers.

54

The reeds ready for rounding.

55

A simple breadboard end, essentially a cross-grain tongue-and-groove joint.

56

A smooth, perfect breadboard end.

57

Preparing the desk lid for breadboard ends.

58

The lower rabbet engages the edges of the case, while the upper rabbets become a moulding after being rounded off.

onto the lopers, the lid serves as the writing surface. Consequently, both sides of the lid must be smooth and attractive. To aid in the battle against warping, the lid includes breadboard ends (**Photo 55**).

Prepare the stock for the lid to at least a Class II surface and be careful that the panel and the two breadboards are a consistent thickness. The breadboard ends should be 1½" wide and will overlap the panel ½" by means of a tongue-and-groove joint. In addition, the lid is rabbeted on the underside, along the top and side edges, which lets it fit into the case and be locked. The top rabbet must fit the case closely in order for the lock to work successfully.

Start making the lid by crosscutting the central panel 1" longer than the desk opening is wide. Make sure to mark all joinery from the interior faces of the wood. If done carefully on carefully prepared stock,

both faces of the breadboard should end up flush with the respective panel faces (**Photo 56**). Mark and cut a tongue on each end that is ¼" thick by ½" long, offset toward the top of the panel to allow the deep rabbet to be cut on the back side. This tongue will engage a similar groove in the breadboards. Plow that groove now (**Photo 57**).

When attaching the breadboards, apply glue only to the center 4" of the tongue. That way the breadboards will stay in place, keeping the lid flat, yet allow the panel to expand and contract without cracking.

With the lid assembled and the breadboards cut flush at the ends, cut the rabbets that engage with the case. Test fit the lid to make sure it will close completely. Then cut the mouldings that run around the outside face (**Photo 58**). There will be some end grain to profile on the breadboard ends; take your time and work

59

When rounding off the lid moulding, remember that the end grain of the breadboard may want to split. Shallow cuts and a sharp plane will help.

60

A small router plane and a gimlet makes quick work of installing the hinges.

61

A peg in each loper will stop you from pulling them out too far. Do not glue these pegs or you will be unable to make repairs in the future.

62

Plane a decorative bevel on the front edges of the lopers. Plane the cross-grain edges first.

63

Random-width pine boards are simply nailed into the case rabbets.

with a sharp, lightly set moulding plane to achieve an attractive moulding (**Photo 59**).

With the lid complete, you can mark the mortises for the hinges and the lock. These tasks require careful layout and careful cutting with both saw and chisel to avoid any scars on the desk interior floor or the writing surface. Take your time and do neat work (**Photo 60**).

Temporarily install the hinges and the lock to check fit and action. Correct any mistakes now before you get to the finishing stage. Once you are satisfied with the way the lid works, remove the hinges and lock again and set them aside until later.

With the lid completed, make the lopers to fit the openings that were left when working on the drawer dividers. To stop them from pulling all the way out, simply drill a ⅜" hole and install a short dowel to act as a stop (**Photo 61**). Do not glue the dowel in place as you want to be able to remove the lopers if needed.

With a pencil, mark a ⅛" line around the end of each loper and bevel this off with a plane to make a small raised area in the center (**Photo 62**).

Once you have the case lid finished, make and fit the ⅜"-thick back boards. These are nailed into the case rabbet with cut nails after you apply the finish to the project (**Photo 63**).

Drill for the pulls

The last step in construction is to install the hardware. Working with Horton Brasses products, I used H-34 drawer pulls, with post-and-nut fittings; H-34E escutcheons; and H-42 knobs for the interior drawers and lopers, all in the "Light Antique" finish.

After all of your hard work building this piece, it's critical that the drawer pulls line up. The best way I know to ensure this is to make a template for the pull posts (**Photo 64**). Simply align the ends of the template with the ends of the drawer and push a pencil through the holes. This will leave an indelible mark at each boring location.

To align the pulls on the three bottom drawers, drill the top one and use a framing square to carry down the boring locations to each of the others. This ensures that all the pulls will line up with each other (**Photo 65**).

Choose a finish

The original period piece upon which this desk is based was stained to resemble mahogany. However, I like the more rural look of the figured maple on its own without the stain. To achieve the finish shown here, I flooded the outer surfaces of the desk twice with boiled linseed oil, allowing it to soak in for 10 to 15 minutes each time before wiping off the excess. Be sure to properly dispose of the oily rags. Linseed oil has a yellowing effect on lighter-colored woods, so to counteract that I used a dewaxed garnet shellac as a top coat. The warm reddish tint will help the maple age into a honey color over time.

I applied seven coats of the shellac, rubbing the dried finish with steel wool after every other coat. Then I rubbed out the final coat with a dark brown paste wax and 0000 steel wool, knocking off some of the shine and letting a bit of "grunge" build up in the corners and creases. This adds significant age to the piece (**Photo 66**). If you'd rather the piece look brand new, simply substitute a light colored paste wax for the final step.

After finishing, re-install the desk lid hinges and the lock mortise. Predrill and screw in the knobs on the lopers and each small drawer in the desk interior. Nail the escutcheons onto each drawer and on the drop lid.

Finally, find a comfortable chair, pull out the lopers, pull down the desk top, and write a letter by hand. It is a lost pleasure, and one that is certainly improved by using a Queen Anne writing desk.

64 Make a template for installing the drawer pulls.

65 A quick and easy way to align hardware in the full-width drawers is to bore the holes in the top drawer and use a framing square to carry the outside hole location down to the other two drawer fronts.

66 A little grunge in a finish adds age. Skip this step if you want to make a new-looking piece.

QUEEN ANNE DESK

OVERALL DIMENSIONS: 20⅞" DEEP X 29½" WIDE X 41" TALL

Qty	Part	Dimensions (inches)			Stock	Comments
		Thickness	Width	Length		
2	Case sides	¾	20¼	38	maple	
1	Case top	¾	9⁵⁄₁₆	28	maple	
1	Case bottom	⅞	19⅞	28¼	pine	
1	Case back	⅜	27½	38	pine	Random-width boards
1	Case lid	⅞	15⅜	25½	maple	½" tongues on both ends
2	Case lid breadboards	⅞	1½	15⅜	maple	
1	Interior front floor board	⅞	11½	27½	maple	
1	Interior rear floor board	⅞	9½	27½	maple	Elevate w/½"-thick blocks to lip front
2	Lopers	⅞	4¼	20	maple	
2	Loper side supports	1	¾	5	maple	
1	Top drawer divider	⅞	1½	27½	maple	
2	Middle & lower drawer dividers	⅞	2³⁄₁₆	27½	maple	
2	Middle & lower drawer runners	⅞	1	17¹¹⁄₁₆	maple	
1	Bottom drawer runner strip*	1	2	62	maple	Oversized; cut to fit on front & sides
1	Base blank	¾	6	72	maple	Miter to fit; cut feet; add glue blocks
1	Rear baseboard	¾	3	29½	pine	

GALLERY

Qty	Part	Thickness	Width	Length	Stock	Comments
4	Interior vertical drawer dividers	⁵⁄₁₆	9¾	8¹⁵⁄₁₆	maple	
4	Side horizontal drawer dividers	³⁄₁₆	7⁵⁄₁₆	8¹⁵⁄₁₆	maple	
1	Central horizontal drawer divider	³⁄₁₆	8⅛	7½	maple	
4	Side drawer fronts	¾	2¼**	7³⁄₁₆	maple	**2¹⁄₁₆ for upper side gallery drawers
4	Side drawer backs	¼	1¹⁵⁄₁₆	7³⁄₁₆	pine	
8	Side drawer sides	¼	2¼**	8¼	pine	**2¹⁄₁₆ for upper side gallery drawers
4	Side drawer bottoms	⅛	8¼	6¹⁵⁄₁₆	pine	
1	Central drawer front	¾	2⁹⁄₁₆	7¼	maple	
1	Central drawer back	¼	2⁷⁄₁₆	7¼	pine	
2	Central drawer sides	¼	2⁹⁄₁₆	7⅝	pine	
1	Central drawer bottom	⅛	7¼	7	pine	
4	Pigeonhole scrollwork	³⁄₁₆	1³⁄₁₆	3⁹⁄₁₆	maple	
2	Pigeonhole vertical dividers	³⁄₁₆	4¾	8⅞	maple	
2	Letter drawer fronts	¾	1¾	9⁷⁄₁₆	maple	
2	Letter drawer backs	½	1¾	9⁷⁄₁₆	pine	
4	Letter drawer sides	¼	7¾	9³⁄₁₆	pine	
2	Letter drawer bottoms	¼	1¾	7¾	pine	

LOWER DRAWERS

Qty	Part	Thickness	Width	Length	Stock	Comments
1	Top drawer front	¾	4⅝	24¼	maple	
1	Top drawer back	½	3⅞	23½	pine	
2	Top drawer sides	½	4¼	18	pine	
1	Top drawer bottom	¼	17⅞	22½	pine	
1	Second top drawer front	¾	5⅜	27½	maple	
1	Second drawer back	½	4⅝	26¾	pine	
2	Second drawer sides	½	5	18	pine	
3	Drawer bottoms	¼	17⅞	25¾	pine	
1	Third drawer front	¾	6⅜	27½	maple	
1	Third drawer back	½	5⅝	26¾	pine	
2	Third drawer sides	½	6	18	pine	
1	Bottom drawer front	¾	7¼	27½	maple	
1	Bottom drawer back	½	6½	26¾	pine	
2	Bottom drawer sides	½	6⅞	18	pine	

* Make up difference between top of case bottom & top of bracket moulding which must completely cover the case dovetails, making the base stick up about 1" into the opening. Note: Rough cut all parts oversize then cut to fit.

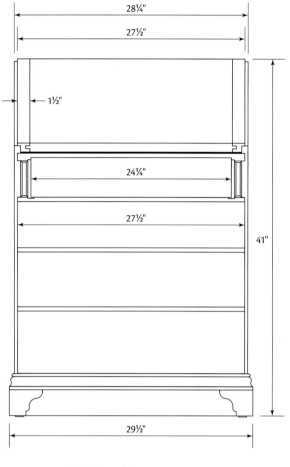

28¼"

27½"

1½"

24¼"

27½"

41"

29½"

**ELEVATION – WITH
DRAWER FRONTS & LID**

20¼"

9½"

4⅝"

5⅜"

6⅜"

7¼"

1⅞"

3"

4"

20⅞"

PROFILE

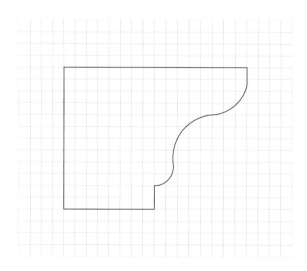

FRONT FOOT PATTERN
One square = ¼"

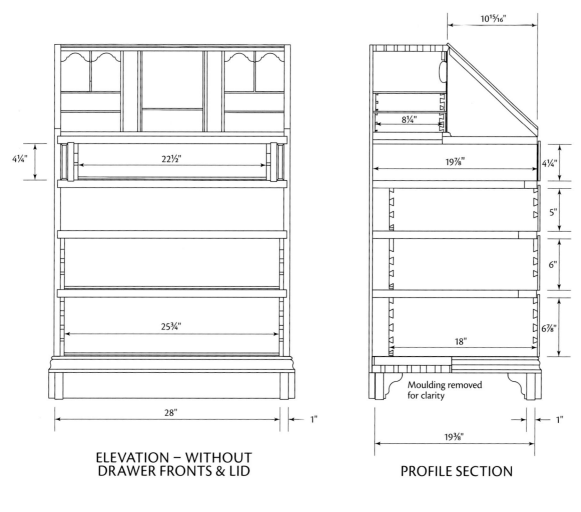

ELEVATION – WITHOUT DRAWER FRONTS & LID

PROFILE SECTION

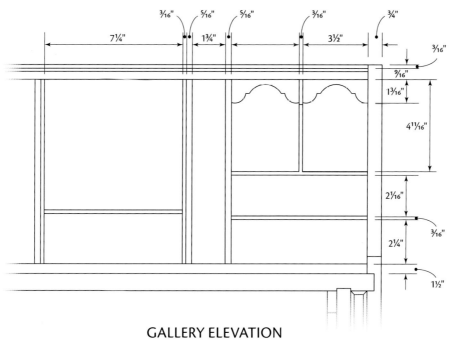

GALLERY ELEVATION

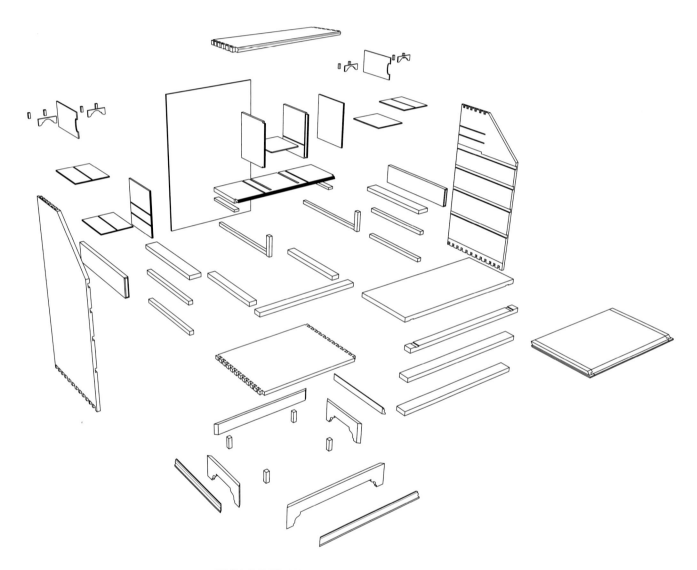

EXPLODED VIEW – WITHOUT DRAWERS

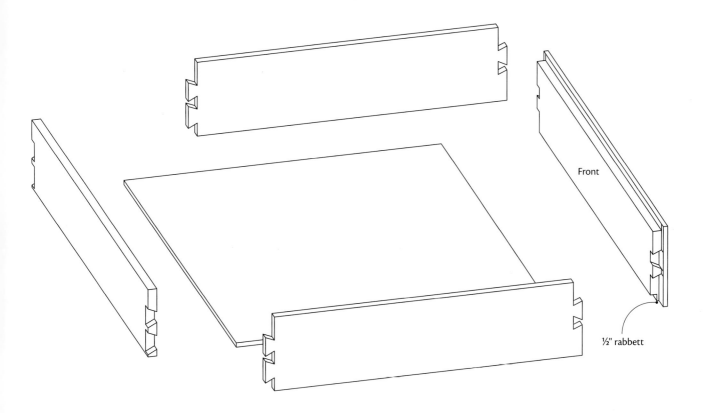

Front

½" rabbett

**DRAWER – EXPLODED VIEW SHOWING
FRONT RABBETT**

CHAPTER SEVEN

Chippendale Bookcase
c. 1770

Although often used as a catch-all reference to rococo furniture made in England and the Colonies, "Chippendale" technically refers to pieces inspired by the work of Thomas Chippendale and his seminal work, "The Gentleman & Cabinetmaker's Director." First published in 1754 and again in an expanded version in 1762, the book contains designs for numerous pieces of furniture, many of which exhibit an Asian influence. In England Chippendale was one of the most famous cabinetmakers of his age, and he also became known throughout America as well, especially in large cities like Philadelphia and New York.

American craftsman were influenced greatly by Chippendale, but as was the case with many trends from the mother country, his designs were blended with other aesthetic influences, in ways that varied by region. In fact, the Chippendale period represents the first major stylistic divergence between New England, Philadelphia and the South.

The overwhelming wealth of Philadelphia allowed its residents to indulge in conspicuous consumption, most notably elaborate ornamental carving, whereas the New England Chippendale pieces retained the pure lines and elegant proportions of Queen Anne, while adopting some of the Chinese elements seen in The Director. Outside the city centers, rural craftsmen borrowed elements of the style but crafted something even more unique, while the Southern furniture powerhouses of Charleston and Savannah had close connections with England and developed an especially pure version of Chippendale's work.

I chose this Pennsylvania piece to represent the Chippendale style for several reasons. Its clean lines and elegant details are characteristic of American Chippendale furniture, but its simple form and bracket feet reflect how regional craftsmen adapted urban styles. Second, the compact design works well in the modern household, where it won't dominate a room with short ceilings, and its simplicity means you won't hesitate to build more than one. In fact, the original this piece is based on is one half of a pair that flanked a small library table.

My wife appreciated this little bookcase so much that I have been "commissioned" to make three more for our library, and perhaps even another pair for our baby daughter Abigail's room.

I also chose this design because of its adaptability. For more on that, see "Elevating the style" at the end of this chapter.

And finally, this design is our first in cherry, a fantastic wood for hand-tool woodworking, and one commonly used in the Chippendale period.

Prep the case parts

I purchased all of the curly cherry for this piece from one flitch, meaning it was all sawed from one tree and kept together from the forest to the lumberyard. This gave me the best chance to make a piece that has consistent color, as the color of cherry can vary widely from tree to tree.

Start by prepping cherry boards for the case sides and shelves, plus a secondary wood for the top and bottom, to approximately ¾" thick and just slightly oversize in both length and width. Since the case bottom and top are completely hidden by the base and a thinner upper top panel, I used pine for those parts. The reference edge for the case parts is the front edge; the reference face is the inside of the case since that is where it needs to be flat for joinery.

The drawer at the bottom of the bookcase slides into an opening formed by the lowest shelf and the bottom of the case.

Once you have the sides ready, lay out the ½"-by-¼" rabbets for the back tboards with a marking gauge. Then lay out the shelf dados, which are ⅜" by ⅜". These narrow dados will receive a tongue on the end of the shelves, formed by cutting a rabbet. I chose that arrangement because it ensures a good fit in the joints, regardless of the thickness of the individual shelves.

As always, clamp the sides together and mark the dado locations at the same time (**Photo 1**). Use a square and knife to scribe the shoulders across the inside faces, and then use a marking gauge to scribe

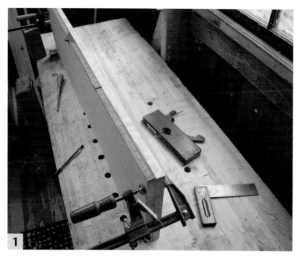

1

As always with case pieces, clamp the sides together and lay out the shelf joinery on both sides simultaneously.

2

Carry the lines across the interior face, square to the reference edge. As a final check, put the back edges of the case together and see if the lines match up.

3

I used a dado plane to form these narrow dados. A fence guides the dado plane.

4

With the dados cut, plane the rabbets for the back boards using a rabbet plane or moving fillister.

the ⅜" depth on the front edges (**Photo 2**). You could saw and chisel these dados as we did in Chapter 2, but I had a sharp dado plane on hand that was a good size for the dados needed, so I used it, guiding it with a long fence (**Photo 3**).

With the dados done, plane the rabbets for the back boards with either a moving fillister or a rabbet plane (**Photo 4**). The rabbets will clear away any damage at the back exits of the dados.

Dovetail the case

With the rabbets and dados cut, you can join the case. The top and bottom are attached to the sides with through dovetails. The tails should be on the hori-

5

The case dovetails: big, clunky and hidden. Speed is the name of the game here.

Chiseling out the waste from the pin board (case side).

zontal boards, so they'll keep the case together when it is loaded with books and the downward force of the shelf loads tries to push the case sides apart.

These dovetails will be hidden, so as you did with the desk, make quick yet functional joints (**Photo 5**). A few gaps here and there are perfectly period correct and will not compromise the strength or aesthetics of the piece.

Our stock was prepared by hand, which will affect the dovetail layout. To take any thickness variations into account, scribe the thickness of each board directly onto its mate, rather than relying on a marking gauge. With this exception, follow the techniques described in Chapter 2 to complete the dovetails and join the case (**Photo 6**).

With case dry-assembled but not yet glued, measure the distances between corners and adjust the fit of the joinery as necessary until the measurements are equal (**Photo 7**). When you're satisfied, disassemble the pieces and smooth the case sides with your smoothing plane. Then you can glue the case together, again checking that it's square as the glue dries.

Dry-assemble the case to check it for square.

Add the top moulding

The pine top board, which is dovetailed into the case, is really a false top, and won't be visible when viewing the piece from the outside. After glue blocks go on top of the case to attach the mouldings, a ¼"-thick piece of cherry (resawed from the same flitch as the rest of the case) is glued down on top of the blocks, hiding them and the pine top from sight.

Choose straight-grained stock for the top mouldings, and cut the profile shown on the measured drawing using the techniques described in Chapter 3. Then miter the moulding at the corners, establish a good, tight fit between the front piece and the side pieces, and then glue and nail the glue blocks to the case and glue the mouldings to the case, driving the nails into the glue blocks only (**Photo 8**). As always, I use cut nails, even when fine nails or brads are called for.

Mould the shelves and attach them

As mentioned earlier, the shelves have a tongue rabbeted onto their ends, which runs the full width of the shelf. I used a moving fillister plane to create this rabbet, which goes on the lower edge of the shelves (**Photo 9**). Adjust the tongue as needed to get a tight fight in the dados, and then plane the shelves to final width (the width of the case side minus the depth of the rabbet at the back). Next, I beaded the front edge of the shelves using a ⁵⁄₁₆" bead plane (**Photo 10**).

8

Glue blocks reinforce the top mouldings.
A few nails never hurt anyone.

9

When rabbeting the underside of the shelves to form a tongue, be sure to use only the reference side (top face) for layout. This ensures the shelf will fit the dado regardless of the its thickness.

10

Plane double beads on the front edges of the shelves.

11

Test-fit the shelves.

12

Check the fit of the miters on the base moulding.

13

Organize the parts for the dovetailed bracket feet.

To attach the shelves, apply glue and slide each shelf in place, being careful to line up the rear edge with the rear rabbet, and apply clamps across the case. Glue the entire width of the shelf into the case dado, as the grain of the wood in the shelves and case is aligned and all of the parts will shrink and expand in the same direction (**Photo 11**).

Add the base moulding and bracket feet

Just like the Queen Anne desk, this bookcase has bracket feet but actually rests on glue blocks that protrude ⅛" below. And as before, the glue blocks have a number of important jobs: They carry the weight of the case and absorb any damage when it is moved. They also help hold the base's corner joints together. The differences here are that the bracket feet are four separate assemblies, with a moulding applied to the case just above them. Also, the bracket joints are dovetails, not miters.

Make and attach the moulding first. Select a piece of cherry that is as straight-grained as possible. It should

be wide enough to cover the lower case dovetails, and long enough to give you enough moulding to wrap around the case with a few inches to spare. Following the moulding practices described previously, mould the blank to the required profile as shown in the measured drawing. Then cut miter joints, fit the pieces to the case, and attach them using glue and brads (the cut variety) (**Photo 12**).

Next, cut the bracket profile onto eight cherry blanks. I used a bowsaw to do this. Smooth the cuts with rasps and sandpaper before using through dovetails to turn the eight pieces into four feet (**Photo 13**). Now flip the case onto its back, leaving its bottom end sticking out over the edge of the bench, and attach the feet to the case with glue blocks. You should also spread glue on the top edge of the feet and clamp them to the bottom of the base moulding. And finally, cut the long glue blocks that go in the corners and protrude ⅛" below the feet, round their ends to prevent splitting, and glue them in also (**Photo 14**).

Dress up the case edges

The last moulding covers the front edges of the case sides, covering up the shelf dados and dressing up these otherwise-plain edges. It matches the mouldings cut on the shelf edges, but is applied to the case after the fact.

Working on the edge of a board, make a length of ¾"-wide double-bead moulding from cherry. This can be done using the same profiled scraper used to bead the William & Mary chair, or by using a ⁵⁄₁₆" beading plane. Rip the first moulding free from the blank, and then mould the edge again and rip it to form the second moulding. Cut these mouldings to fit between the base and top mouldings, then attach them with glue and cut brad nails.

Make the drawer

Cut and fit another piece of curly cherry to serve as the drawer front. It should be planed to fit tightly into the drawer opening. Plane a ⁵⁄₁₆"-deep by ⅝"-wide rabbet into the bottom inside edge; this is where the drawer bottom will be nailed. Next, prepare the ⅝"-thick stock for your drawer sides to the height of the drawer front and cut a ⁵⁄₁₆"-deep by ⅜"-wide rabbet on the bottom edge of each piece. Then crosscut and plane the pieces to their final lengths with a backsaw and shooting board. Make the rear drawer piece the same height as the drawer sides minus ⁵⁄₁₆", as the rear piece does not have the rabbet (the bottom is nailed directly onto the lower edge).

The drawer has half-blind dovetails at the front and through-dovetails at the back. Cut your dovetails using the techniques described in Chapter 2, and focus on achieving a tight, attractive joint for the half-blinds at the front. Cut, fit and nail in the drawer bottoms and then glue on the drawer slips. Finally, test the operation and fit of the drawer and adjust as necessary. Bore the holes for the drawer pulls and cut the lock mortise in the drawer front.

A clear finish is best

I managed to purchase cherry that was all from the same tree. Otherwise I might have had to add a pains-taking step to the finishing process: staining the boards to match each other. If you can find wide cherry boards (to avoid a glue line) from the same flitch, with minimal sapwood (I had only one small streak that I was able to "hide" inside the case), the finishing process will be quite easy. I simply used five coats of blonde shellac, which I then rubbed out with dark brown paste wax. This gave the curly cherry a chance to really shine without being muddied by layers of pigments or glazes.

After finishing the case, the last woodworking operation is to cut and fit the ¼"-thick, random-width pine back boards. These are nailed into the case rabbets.

Hardware from Horton

This piece calls for two Horton Brasses H-34 drawer pulls (I like the post-and-nut fittings for pulls like this). As usual, I used the "Light Antique" finish on the brass, though you may choose from a number of different finishes ("Bright" would be my second choice). Install the hardware after the finishing and rub-out, and make sure to wipe your fingerprints off the brass (one of my pet peeves!).

With that done, select just the right spot in your house, load up the shelves with your favorite books, curios or antiques, and marvel at your work.

Elevating the style

The scope of this book limits the complexity of the projects. While this bookcase is a simplified Chippendale form, others of the period featured scrolled tops with a "gooseneck moulding." If you prefer this look, it won't be difficult to adapt the top of this case to the task. But you may wish to make the case itself several feet taller, perhaps 6 or 7 ft. total, or the proportions of the scrolled top could make the piece look very heavy and out of place. And if you make a taller case, it would be a good idea to attach the shelves with sliding dovetail joints (rather than simple dados) as this will help keep the case together when it's loaded with even more books.

Another fun feature to add is a hidden drawer, called a map drawer, which slides into the space between the false pine top and the thin cherry top above it. The front piece of the mitered moulding then acts as a drawer front.

One last interesting possibility is to use maple rather than cherry, eliminate the bracket base, and modify the width and depth, turning the bookcase into a secretary top for the Queen Anne desk in Chapter 6. In that case, you might add doors.

14

It looks a little funky, but this is spot-on period construction. Lots of glue blocks.

CHIPPENDALE BOOKCASE

OVERALL DIMENSIONS: 11¾" DEEP X 29½" WIDE X 45⅛" TALL

Qty	Part	Thickness	Width	Length	Stock	Comment
			Dimensions (inches)			
		Thickness	Width	Length	Stock	Comment
2	Case sides	¾	11	41⅛	cherry	
1	Case bottom	¾	10¾	28	pine	
1	False case top	¾	11	28	pine	
1	Case top	¼	11	28	cherry	
1	Top case moulding	¾	1¾	60	cherry	Make in one length, miter & cut to fit; reinforce with glue blocks
6	Curved bracket foot pieces	¾	3	4	cherry	
2	Angled bracket foot pieces	¾	3	4	cherry	
4	Glue blocks	1	1	3	pine	
1	Base moulding	¾	¾	60	cherry	Make in one length, miter & cut to fit
3	Shelves	¾	10⅝	27¼	cherry	
1	Drawer front	¾	3⅝	26½	cherry	
2	Drawer sides	½	3⅝	8¾	pine	
1	Drawer back	½	3⁵⁄₁₆	26½	pine	
1	Drawer bottom	¼	8½	25½	pine	
	Case back	¼	40⅜	27½	pine	Shiplapped random-width boards
1	Double-beaded face frame moulding	⁵⁄₁₆	¾	170	cherry	Cut to fit

Note: Rough cut all parts oversize then cut to fit.

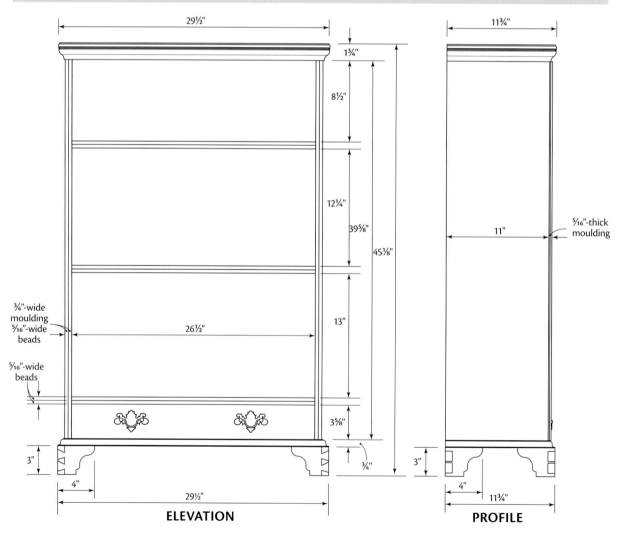

ELEVATION

PROFILE

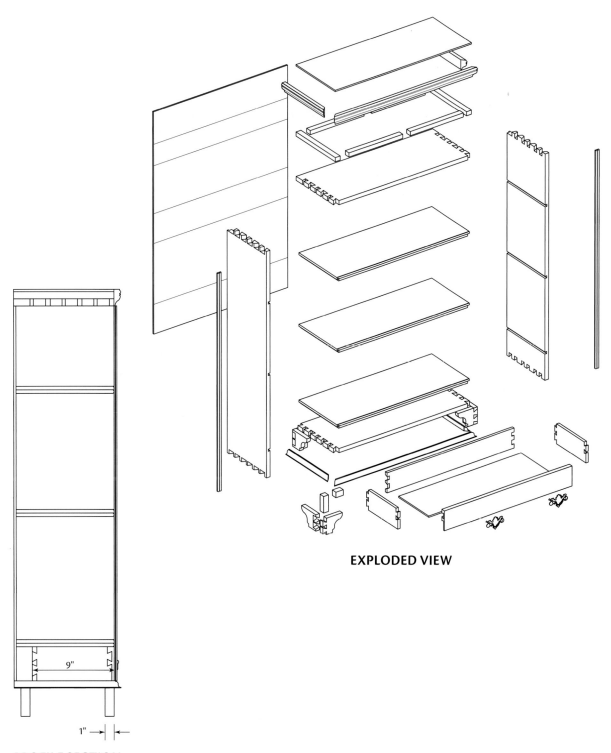

EXPLODED VIEW

9"

1"

PROFILE SECTION

CHAPTER EIGHT

Hepplewhite Huntboard
c. 1810

The neoclassical style of the Federal period was a direct result of the archaeological digs at Pompeii and Herculaneum, which commenced in 1738 and generated great public interest. The discoveries at these sites inspired a generation of architects, furniture makers and engravers, many of whom saw the digs firsthand on a young gentleman's "Grand Tour" of Europe.

This phenomenon brought about a sea change in English furniture, as men such as Robert Adam, Thomas Sheraton and George Hepplewhite blended classical forms of the ancient world with modern sensibilities to create something new. Today, we use the term "Federal" as a generic reference to the work of these men.

In the newly created United States of America, the ideals of the Greeks and Romans were especially popular, as we sought to establish an identity separate from England. Many of the founding principles of this country can be traced directly to these ancient societies, so it makes sense that the design motifs favored during this time of upheaval would spring from the same source.

American craftsman, as was typical, adapted the work of English designers, specifically those presented in George Hepplewhite's "The Cabinet Maker and Upholsterer's Guide," first published in 1788, and Thomas Sheraton's "The Cabinet Maker and Upholsterer's Drawing Book" of 1791. Eschewing the more elaborate designs of Robert Adam, American craftsman created neoclassical furniture forms with simplified lines and delicate proportions. They decorated these high-style pieces with elaborate veneer and inlay patterns, leaving behind the carved decoration of rococo and rendering the Chippendale style obsolete.

As the economic power of the United States increased, the new wealth was showcased in expensive veneered surfaces. This small Vermont Hepplewhite sideboard, however, like the Pennsylvania Chippendale bookcase, shows how rural craftsmen adapted high urban styles. The man who made the original adopted Hepplewhite's huntboard design, its proportions, and its classic tapered leg profile, but executed it in domestic walnut rather than expensive (and perhaps unobtainable) exotic veneers, and then used bead treatments on the legs and drawers to dress up the otherwise plain piece.

The result is an understated yet classic piece of Federal-era American furniture that will introduce you to the style without the most daunting veneer and inlay work. That said, you'll learn plenty of new techniques here, including basic veneering for the case sides, how to taper and bead legs, and how to build veneered, beaded drawers.

Prepping your stock

This piece doesn't require a lot of primary wood. The drawers are poplar, with walnut veneered onto their fronts. The top front stretcher, the back and the case sides (also veneered with walnut) are pine.

As you did for the Queen Anne stool, make sure that the grain on the leg blanks runs from corner to corner. This ensures that each leg will have a consistent grain pattern on its two show faces.

And as always with case pieces, the most important step in preparing stock is ensuring that the two reference faces are flat, straight and square to each other. This is especially important in a piece like this, where the strength of the overall construction is determined by the fit between the case sides and the legs. Also important here is to plane the leg blanks to a consistent 1½" square (or 1¾" square if you like a sturdier-looking leg). The legs will be both tapered and beaded, and any variation from square will be obvious in the final piece. Remember to mark your two reference faces and to measure only from those faces (**Photo 1**).

Part of the stock preparation is veneering the sides of the case. Plane the pine stock to approximately ¾" thick. Ensure that the outside face, the one that will be veneered, is as flat and smooth as possible.

This is a natural place to use the hammer veneer technique, using hot hide glue, but I had just purchased an antique book press and wanted to try it out. I spread

I like to use chalk to mark dark woods like walnut. Pencil would be nearly invisible.

I used a book press to veneer the sides of the case. Hammer veneering would also work well.

Trim the veneer flush with the edges. There's no real need to veneer the bottom edge or the interior face, though you can if you choose.

liquid hide glue on each face to be veneered, then placed a sheet of veneer on the glue. I then made the following sandwich for clamping both sides at once: side panel (veneer up), wax paper, side panel (veneer down), clamping cauls, then a pushing block (**Photo 2**). Once the glue was dry, I removed the panels from the press and trimmed up the veneer with a knife and a sharp block plane (**Photo 3**).

Plane the wide pine board for the case back to approximately ¾" thick, leaving it oversized in width

and length for fitting later. The front upper stretcher is also ¾"-thick pine.

Also prepare the ¾"-thick lower stretcher, which must be walnut – as it will be visible in the final piece. And last, glue up the center divider, which is a ¾"-thick pine board (I used two pieces to make up the width) with walnut edging at the front. The grain on this panel must run top-to-bottom, as it will ultimately be attached to the case top with glue blocks and will need to expand and contract with it.

Multiple mortise-and-tenons join the sides and back

Pick the leg blanks with the most attractive grain for the front legs, marking them as shown in Chapter 6. Plane the case sides to their final width, clamp them together, and then lay out the tenon shoulders on both pieces at the same time (**Photo 4**). This helps to ensure that the case will turn out square. Mark out the thickness of the tenons using a marking gauge (be sure to offset the tenon away from the veneered face), then use the same setting to lay out the mortises on the legs (**Photo 5**).

For this piece, it makes sense to cut the tenons before the mortises. We'll do that to join the sides to the legs, and then add the back later.

Using a crosscut backsaw and a straightedge clamped to the workpiece, saw the shoulder of the tenons (**Photo 6**). Now mark the width of the three tenons on each end, and saw them out using a rip-filed backsaw. Remove the waste between them with a coping saw, bowsaw or simply by chopping with a chisel. Then trim the tenons to final length.

4

The sides and back join the legs with multiple tenons. Lay out the shoulders simultaneously. Pardon the newfangled clamps – I ran out of old ones!

5

The tenon thickness should be roughly ⅜", but match it to whatever mortising chisel you intend to use.

6

A fence clamped to the layout line enables you to cut clean and precise tenon shoulders with a backsaw.

7

The best way to lay out the mortises is to scribe them directly from the tenons.

8

Dry-clamp the case sides to test the fit of the joinery.

With multiple tenons in a row, it makes sense to lay out the mortises directly from the tenons. Be sure that the top edge of the case side aligns with the top end of each leg before scribing the tenon locations onto the leg (**Photo 7**). With that done, chop all your leg mortises and then test the fit of each joint, paying close attention to the fit at the shoulders (**Photo 8**). Also, the veneered face of each case side should be flush with the outside of each leg; if they are not, make adjustments as needed.

Now repeat this mortise and tenon process for the case back. Clamp the case together to ensure that the assembly is square before moving on. This is best done by measuring from the front right corner to the back left, and then repeating the measurement from the front left to the back right.

9

Sizing the top front stretcher. The secret to accurate hand work is to scribe parts to each other whenever possible, rather than measuring.

Dividers let you establish an even shoulder on both edges without measuring.

The dovetail layout on the top front stretcher.

Make the shoulder cuts first, as shown, and then saw the angled sides.

Rabbet the dovetail to ⅜" thick.

Cut joinery for the front rails

Before taking the case apart, check again that the sides are still square to the back and then lay the pine stock for the top front stretcher on the top of the front legs, with the front edges aligned. Scribe lines at the outside faces of the legs (**Photo 9**). Now draw lines ¾" farther in the first pencil lines. These new lines establish the ends of the dovetails that will hold the stretcher in place. Cut the stretcher off at these new lines, and then lay out and cut the dovetail (**Photos 10-12**). Reduce the tail to ⅜" thickness, as this will make cutting the socket in each leg much less labor intensive (**Photo 13**).

Now place the stretcher back on the leg tops, ensuring that the front edge of the stretcher aligns exactly with the leg fronts, and scribe around the dovetails onto the end grain of each leg (**Photo 14**). Once the dovetail

Place the top rail onto the front legs to transfer the dovetail layout onto them.

Detail of the layout for the dovetail socket in the legs.

15

16

Saw past the top layout line and then dig in the toe of the saw with short strokes to reach the inside corner.

17

Chop out the waste.

18

Concentrate on achieving a good fit at the front edge; the interior shoulder is less important.

19

Dry-clamp the assembly and flip it over to mark the location of the mortise for the bottom stretcher and determine the stretcher's length.

sockets are scribed, mark their depth also, and then saw and chop the sockets as shown (**Photos 15-18**).

The lower front stretcher is joined to the front legs with a "barefaced" mortise-and-tenon joint, which is open on one side. With the case dry-assembled and set upside down on the bench, place the lower stretcher on the case sides. Scribe pencil lines on the stretcher where it meets the inside of the legs, and also mark a line on the legs that represents the bottom of the case sides (**Photo 19**). Next, cut the stretcher to length, including the tenon lengths, and then cut ⅜"-thick tenons on each end, cutting the shoulders just on the waste side of the pencil line you just scribed.

The bottom of the front stretcher will be aligned with the bottom of the case sides, so the bottom of its

20

The mortise for the bottom stretcher is open on one side. Saw inside the layout lines and prepare to chop the waste.

21

The completed mortise.

mortise is the pencil line you scribed earlier. The top is marked from the tenon to ensure a good fit. Mark the length of the tenon onto the leg face, then cut the top and bottom mortise lines with a crosscut backsaw, ensuring that you don't go past either of the two depth lines (**Photo 20**). With that completed, remove the waste from the mortise with a chisel, testing the fit of the joint at regular intervals (**Photo 21**).

The center divider needs room for movement

Dry-assemble the case and check for square one more time. Once you are satisfied, get ready to add the center divider, which is really a full center panel inside the case. The grain of this panel runs vertically, so it can be attached firmly to the top of the huntboard, which will move in the same direction. But the grain in the case's side panels runs horizontally, meaning the case won't move front to back. So the center divider is tenoned into the back of the case, but wedged instead of glued, with extra room left at the tenon shoulders for seasonal wood movement.

To lay out the joinery at the back, start at the front. Mark a pencil line on the lower front stretcher at the exact midpoint between the front legs. Using a square, carry this line onto the top face of the stretcher, and then up onto the top stretcher. Now, using a framing square, carry this line to the case back and make a mark. Draw a line at this mark with a square, referencing off the bottom edge of the case back. Offset this line about ⅜" to the right and again make a vertical line down the case back, square to the bottom. That represents one side of the mortises. Now offset this second line to the left ¾" jumping over your original marks (**Photo 22**). These lines represent the outside edges of three mortises for the central drawer divider. Now widen the mortises ⅜" on one side to accommodate the opposing wedges that will anchor the tenons while letting them move in and out with the seasons (**Photo 23**).

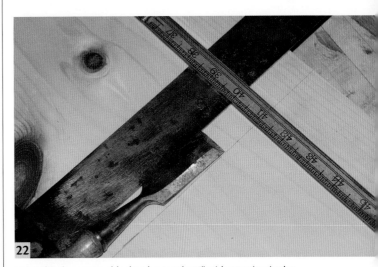

22

Use a chisel as a gauge block to lay out the ¾"-wide mortises in the case back.

23

The wedges, test fit in the case. Note the ⅜" gap between the shoulder of the divider and the case back. This allows the divider to move with the seasons without forcing the case apart.

24

To save expensive walnut, the center divider is glued up from pine and walnut. Notch the front edge to fit between the front case stretchers.

25

Lay out the rear tenons on the central divider.

26

Cut the tenons, and use them to lay out the mortises in the case back. Note the extra ⅜" added to the mortises to accommodate the wedges.

Now you can mark the joinery on the divider itself. Start at the front edge, which is a walnut strip, and mark the distance between the top and bottom front stretchers. Set a marking gauge to the depth of the stretchers and scribe those lines on the walnut strip too. Then use a backsaw to cut to the lines, notching the divider to fit behind the stretchers (**Photo 24**).

Once this is done, measure the distance between the front stretchers and the rear case back. Subtract ⅜" to allow for wood movement, and then scribe that distance on the central divider, measuring from the shoulders of the notches at the front. This line will serve as the shoulder for the divider tenons. Trim the board so that the rear end is approximately 1½" beyond the tenon shoulder line, and then lay out the tenons per the measured drawing (**Photo 25**). Cut them using a rip backsaw and chisel.

With the tenons cut you can transfer their widths and locations onto the back of the case (**Photo 26**).

I bored out most of the mortise waste before trimming to the lines with sharp chisels (**Photo 27**).

Make the wedges from ¾"-thick pine scrap approximately the same width as your mortises and about 2" long. Saw through the thickness at a diagonal to make pairs of wedges (**Photos 28-29**). Keep the matching pairs together by numbering them.

Assemble in stages, as usual

When the wedges are done and you are happy with the fit of the central divider (both the tenons in the back and the shoulders at the front), it's finally time to glue up the case!

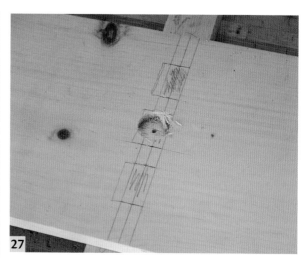

27

Bore out the waste before finishing up with chisels.

Glue up the side assemblies first and allow them to dry overnight. The rest of the glue-up has to happen in one shot. Glue and clamp the rear case back in place, then the lower front stretcher, followed by the central divider. Loosely install the rear wedges, and then glue in the the top stretcher. Moving quickly, place the assembly on the end of your workbench, so you have a solid nailing surface. Then, align the central drawer divider so that it is square with the lower front stretcher and drive a single nail into the end grain of the divider through the top stretcher. Flip the case over and drive another nail into the bottom end grain through the bottom stretcher. Finally, drive the wedges tight. Do not glue them in place; you will want to be able to adjust them over time. Take a breath.

28

Laying out the opposing wedges. The easy way to cut these is to saw the angle and free one wedge, and then make a crosscut to free the remaining one. Then repeat that process.

29

One pair of opposing wedges, the secret to constructing a case that will not self-destruct with seasonal movement.

Once the case is dry, trim the rear wedges and tenons flush with the outside face of the case back so that the piece will sit tight against a wall.

The last major part of the case is the thin top, which is held in place for now with a nail driven down into each leg. I had enough ⅜"-thick walnut for this project

on hand; you may have to resaw a 4/4 board or simply buy some ⅜" stock at the lumberyard. Glue the stock together to a sufficient width, and then cut the top just slightly oversize once the glue is dry.

To attach the top board, align it so it is roughly flush with all four sides of the case. Predrill a small hole through the top over each leg and drive a 1" cut nail into each, setting the head of the nail below the surface (this will later be filled with colored wax). Now take a sharp block plane and carefully plane the top flush to the case, first along its end grain and then the long-grain edges.

Attach the drawer runners and top moulding

The interior structure of the huntboard accomplishes two tasks. For one, it supports the drawers and gives them a smooth track to run on. But it also helps to secure the thin top, as you'll see shortly. Lay down a moving blanket or something similar on your benchtop, and place the huntboard on it, upside-down. The first two drawer runners are placed about halfway up the drawer openings, one at each end of the case, providing a bumper for the drawer sides to run against. To make these, cut strips of pine scrap to fit between the legs, plane them so that the inside edge is flush with the interior surface of the legs, and glue them into place.

Next, glue four strips of ¾" scrap to the bottom of the interior — two against the sides of the case and two against the central divider — ensuring that their top faces are flush with the top of the bottom stretcher (**Photos 30-31**). These strips are the surface that the drawers run on.

Four similarly sized pieces will be used to attach the top to the case sides and the central divider; apply glue only to the front half of the faces that touch the top. To clamp these in place, you can use short, thin pieces of scrap to fashion miniature "go bars," sized so they can be flexed between the lower runners and upper glue blocks. You could also simply use hot hide glue and rub the blocks into place.

Once the interior structure is in place, you can stick, miter, and apply the moulding to the case top. As with virtually all of my period reproduction work – based on my analysis of many originals (including the one in question here) – I used headless brads to attach the mouldings to the case while the glue dries. As always, all nails are the cut variety. Sink them below the surface of the wood and fill them in with colored wax once the piece has been finished (**Photo 32**).

30

Filler strips are glued into the bottom and top of the case for the drawers to run against. The top one (bottom here) helps to hold the top on but is only glued halfway along the top to allow it to move seasonally. The sides of the case also get filler strips glued halfway up the drawer opening.

31

The central drawer runners.

After the top moulding is mitered and attached, the case is ready for drawers.

32

33

Rabbeting the lower interior edge of the drawer fronts prior to crosscutting them apart.

34

The beading applied to the drawer front. Also note the glue blocks which attach the bottom to the drawer.

Beaded, veneered drawers

To ensure a consistent grain pattern and coloration, I chose to veneer the drawer fronts, which was common practice in the period. The front blanks should be poplar, roughly ¾" thick. As you did with the case sides, make the outside faces of these boards as flat and smooth as possible.

Plane the bottom edge of the board flat and square to the front to serve as your reference edge. Then plane a 1"-wide by ⅜" deep rabbet into the back of the drawer front (**Photo 33**). This will enable you to nail in the drawer bottom while leaving extra space below for glue blocks, which helps to keep the bottom in place (**Photo 34**).

Once you have the rabbet cut, saw and plane drawer fronts to fit the case openings. Then veneer the drawer fronts following the same techniques you used on the case sides. When the glue is dry, trim the veneer flush with a sharp knife followed by a block plane.

The drawers are dovetailed together using half blinds at the front and through dovetails at the rear. Cut the dovetails as usual, but be especially careful to protect the drawer front from rough handling since it is veneered.

Because the front is veneered, we need to protect its face and edges from damage in use. This is done by applying cock beading around the drawer faces. This is essentially a ⅜"-by-⅜" beaded strip of wood that is glued into a rabbet on all four edges and mitered at the corners, with the beads sitting proud of the veneered face.

Start by using a No. 6 hollow plane to round over the edge of a long piece of ⅜"-thick walnut. The goal, as with all hand-cut mouldings, is to make a piece of moulding long enough so that all mitered pieces can be cut from one strip, ensuring a consistent look and smooth transitions.

Now set a cutting gauge to ⅜" and, running the fence on the beaded face (being careful not to rock the gauge), slice off the strip of moulding. If you don't have a cutting gauge, you can also saw the piece off; just be extremely careful to avoid breaking the moulding.

The bead should sit proud of the drawer front by about ⅛", so cut a ⅜"-wide by ¼"-deep rabbet into the drawer face, along all four edges (**Photo 35**). Scribe

35

The rabbets for the bead. Make sure to score the veneer completely through prior to removing the waste. If you don't you run the risk of splintering the veneer along the edge.

the ⅜" dimension into the veneered face with a cutting gauge before planing the rabbet, or you risk splintering and tearing the veneer.

After scoring the lines, I use a moving fillister plane to make the rabbet about ⁵⁄₁₆" wide, and then I remove the remaining waste with a shoulder plane. This helps me prevent the above-described (and much dreaded) veneer tearout.

Since its a bit dangerous to plane the veneered face, sand it to #220-grit. Then miter and glue the beading into the rabbets. I use packing tape or duct tape, pulled tightly, to hold the pieces in place while the glue dries. Any tape residue will wipe away with alcohol.

As with all hand-shaped mouldings, the miter joints may require a little touch-up with a sharp chisel or sandpaper to ensure that the beads meet perfectly.

Lay out and drill the drawer fronts for the drawer pulls, and then fit the drawers to the case with a sharp plane (**Photos 36-37**).

Easy way to age walnut

As walnut ages, it often turns from the dark greyish-brown we all love to a reddish-orange color. In fact, old walnut often resembles newly stained mahogany. Replicating this age-lightened look usually involves a number of different dyes and glazes, and multiple layers of shellac. However, I recently stumbled across an easier recipe for this finish in *Popular Woodworking Magazine*, which is nothing more than Transtint dye (the "Reddish Brown" color) mixed into in clear shellac.

I used store-bought shellac, right out of the can, and did not change the "cut" (the thickness of the shellac as adjusted with denatured alcohol). I added approximately 100 drops of the dye to the 1-qt. can before stirring. This will make a lot of finish, but I use a lot of walnut a lot in my work. If you want to make a smaller batch, the article recommends four drops per 2 oz. ounces of shellac.

After four coats of the tinted shellac, I rubbed the piece out with amber paste wax and 0000 steel wool to reduce the sheen, and then filled in the top nail holes with colored wax. I couldn't be happier with the process and the final result. I plan to use this finish to age my walnut projects from now on.

Period-correct possibilities

The piece I chose to reproduce is a very simple version of Hepplewhite, with almost no ornamentation other than the simple mouldings. Many other pieces in the

36

Finding the center of the drawer to lay out the holes for the pull.

37

Using dividers to lay out the drawer pull bolt holes.

Hepplewhite style feature elaborate inlays and exotic wood veneers. While this level of decoration is beyond the scope and intent of "With Saw, Plane & Chisel," it would be entirely appropriate to investigate and use these techniques to dress up the piece.

Alternatively, you could go the opposite way, building the entire piece out of a paint-friendly wood like poplar or pine, and giving it a multi-layer milk- or oil-paint finish similar to the one some Windsor chair-makers use. Painting such a piece would also be period-correct, and would simply move the piece from an urban setting into a rural context. Country Hepplewhite pieces, when painted, have a beautiful appearance that fits into many interiors.

HEPPLEWHITE SIDEBOARD

OVERALL DIMENSIONS: 15¾" DEEP X 43" WIDE X 34⅝" TALL

Dimensions (inches)

Qty	Part	Thickness	Width	Length	Stock	Comments
4	Legs	1½	1½	34¼	walnut	Final dim at top; start w/1¾-square blank
1	Case top	⅜	15	43	walnut	
2	Case sides	¾	9¼	13½	pine w/ walnut veneer	3 ¾" tenons both ends
1	Case top moulding	¾	1⅛	80	walnut	Make one piece, miter to fit
1	Case back	¾	9¼	41½	pine w/ walnut veneer	3 ¾" tenons both ends
1	Lower front stretcher	¾	1½	41½	walnut	¾" tenon both ends
1	Top front stretcher	¾	1½	41½	pine w/ walnut veneer	¾" dovetail both ends
1	Central drawer divider	¾	15	9¼	pine w/ walnut strip	Orientation is vertical, 3 tenons on rear, walnut strip on front
6	Wedges for central divider	⅜	1½	1½	pine	
4	Drawer runners	¾	1¾	12	pine	
2	Case side filler strips	¾	2	12	pine	Fit between legs & glued to case side
4	Top filler strips	¾	1¾	12	pine	
2	Drawer fronts	⅝	7¾	19⅝	poplar w/ walnut veneer	
2	Drawer backs	⅜	7¾	19⅝	poplar	
4	Drawer sides	⅜	7¾	13	poplar	
2	Drawer bottoms	¼	12⅝	18⅞	poplar	
1	Cock beading	⅜	⅜	120	walnut	Make 1 or 2 long pieces, then cut to fit
8	Drawer glue blocks	⅜	¾	4	pine	
1	Drawer long glue block	⅜	¾	18⅞	pine	

Note: Rough cut all parts oversize then cut to fit.

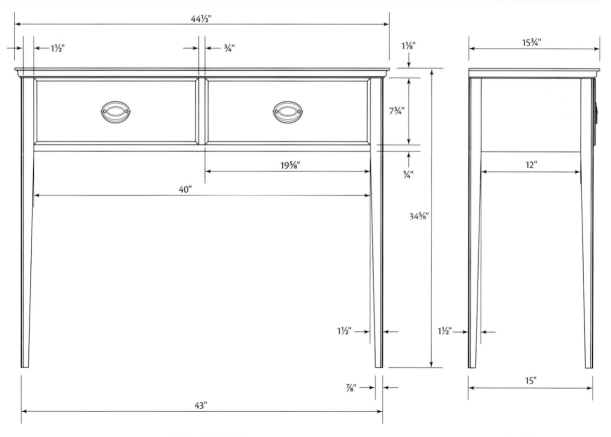

ELEVATION   PROFILE

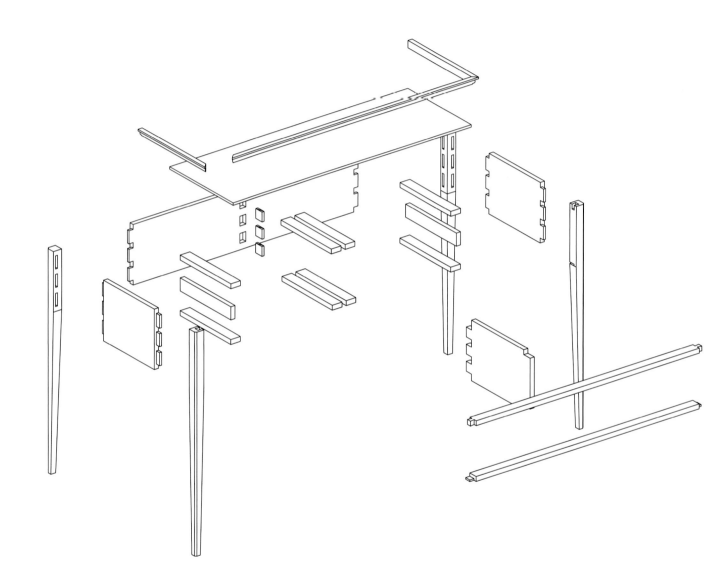

EXPLODED VIEW MINUS DRAWERS

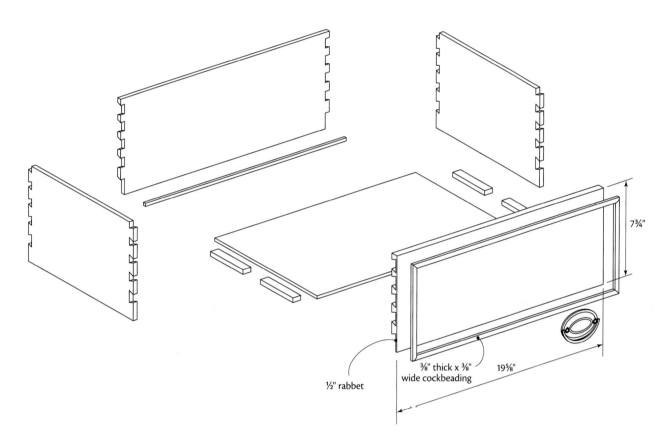

7³⁄₄"

½" rabbet

³⁄₈" thick x ³⁄₈"
wide cockbeading

19⅝"

EXPLODED VIEW – DRAWER DETAILS

THOUGHTS
ON CRAFT

CHAPTER NINE

Lessons Learned

If you have worked through each chapter of "With Saw, Plane & Chisel," and followed the techniques, congratulations! You've learned a number of very useful things. You've learned how to prepare lumber by hand for furniture projects. You've learned traditional joinery, decorative techniques and a bit of upholstery, as well as a brief history of each of the major furniture styles of the 18th century. Most importantly, you've learned how hand-tool work differs from power-tool work. To work efficiently and effectively with hand tools, the process is different, your mindset must be different, and the results are wonderfully different.

While the techniques I've described can be used to make the furniture of any time period, and many can be used in concert with power tools, making period-correct furniture is where the hand-tool paradigm really pays dividends.

In addition to understanding the mindset and techniques used by our craft ancestors, you've seen that it only takes a small collection of tools to reproduce work like theirs. One of the things that amazes tool-obsessed modern woodworkers is that most of an 18th-century cabinetmaker's kit can fit in a box with less volume than a modern file cabinet. Far from being tool hoarders, or to be nicer, "collectors," historic woodworkers owned just enough to get the job done. Tools were expensive (some still are), and unless a craftsman had a well-off family to support him, a la Benjamin Seaton, or a particularly generous master, he followed the old adage: "Use it up, wear it out, make it do, or do without."

The work that period woodworkers were able to accomplish with such a small kit is astonishing when you compare it with the level of tooling in most modern shops, even hobby shops. I hope that you'll see "With Saw, Plane & Chisel" as a gateway to escaping the tool-acquisition trend and focusing on getting better with what you have on hand. Beech is still beech, and steel is, for the most part, still steel. If you train your hand and eye, you can do exactly what woodworkers of the past did, in your own shop of today.

Jack of all trades, master of none

One 18th-century reality that contributed to the high output of period woodworkers, and partially explains their small tool kits, was specialization. Furniture makers often bought wood already sawn close to the proper size and thickness, by professional sawyers, eliminating the need for rough hewing, planing and sawing. A Philadelphia chair maker probably wouldn't have needed carving chisels, as he would have turned the parts over to a professional carver for that work. He likely wouldn't have finished his own chairs or done his own upholstery either. And for his own specialized work, the chair maker would have served an apprenticeship and put in countless hours at the bench to learn to satisfy the demands of an astute clientele.

In contrast, modern woodworkers attempt do the work of several period craftsmen – without their training and experience. So there can be wide variations in skill levels for the various aspects of the work. Even with these limitations, modern woodworkers take on the most challenging and impressive pieces made in the 18th century.

This, in some ways, explains the modern woodworking community and its obsession with tools and equipment. We know we can't be good at everything, so we seek the next great innovation to allow us to cut those crisp dovetails, or carve the perfect Newport shell, or apply a French polish in 20 minutes. Resisting these temptations is difficult, and the search for easy answers makes a great deal of money for some people as they push their own particular dogma or tooling to an eager audience. I propose a bold alternative.

Don't believe everything you read

The Internet is a wonderful tool for those seeking to learn the old ways, and its openness allows anyone, professional or amateur, to publish anything, whereas in the past, masters and apprentices were expected to keep the secrets of their craft.

In the vast expanse of websites and blogs, we devoted hand tool users are the weirdos of the woodworking world. We talk about citric acid rust removal for a moulding plane iron rather than just buying a new router bit. We're the ones who actually try to sharpen our own handsaws instead of just running down to The Borg for a new table saw blade. We like it when our projects actually look like they were made by a human, rather than sporting a series of pristine machined surfaces. Being part of an online community that reinforces that it's OK to be "Beyond the Norm" (to borrow a phrase from Roy Underhill) is a fantastic thing. As with all things, however, there is a dark side.

We read far too many things online that aren't particularly helpful. We see commentary about how perfectly flat the sole must be to make a handplane work properly, despite the reality that many fine craftsmen don't worry about such trivialities. We hear that you can't cut dovetails without a razor-thin side bevel on your chisel, and to heck with what Job Townsend did.

If you wouldn't ask a stranger on an Internet forum what size shirt you should wear, why would you ask them how high your workbench should be? Should I try waterstones? No, use diamond stones! No, oil stones! No, Scary Sharp! Confusion reigns.

The echo chamber of internet woodworking forums is strong. Truths and non-truths reverberate with equal magnitude in the minds of the people who want good information most.

The solution? Escape. Think for yourself! Try things, think about things, make mistakes and make discoveries!

And if you want to be a helpful member of the woodworking community, don't simply quote what Nicholson said, or Roubo, or Hayward, or Moxon, or Klausz. Anyone can read their words for themselves and attempt to adapt them to their work. What is much harder to find than recycled information, and much more valuable, is the true hands-on experience of individual craftsmen, both novice and experienced, who share their knowledge in a constructive way.

If you don't have experience with something, don't wait for someone else to figure it out for you. Try it! Write it up, share it and advance the craft.

The average person will start to believe almost anything if they've been exposed to it enough. Think about how many times you've heard how you must have sharp side bevels on a dovetail chisel. Did you actually try to chop the waste with a firmer chisel as I demonstrated in this book? If you did, I bet you you did just fine with the simpler tool – and that's the point.

I have more respect for the person who tries, fails and shares that failure than the man who tries nothing and knows it all. I hope you feel the same way.

Yours in the fellowship of craft,
Zachary Dillinger

CHAPTER 10

Further Explorations

Since my late teens, one of my greatest obsessions has been accurately reproducing period furniture by hand. Even when I'm not in the shop actively working, my mind is working through joinery problems, planning what to make next, and thinking of different techniques to try. That passion is fed, inspired, and kept burning by discovery. I continue to explore the innumerable variations, tools, techniques and tricks used by our woodworking ancestors. I have presented just a small sample in this book; to pretend that this work is anything other than an introduction to the world of period work would be an injustice.

Consequently, I would like to provide you with a list of my favorite reference books, the works I return to time and again to stoke the fires of creativity. If you are just getting started, these are the first books you should buy – or check out from the local library as I often do (with the help of my wife, April, who happens to be a librarian).

Period references

While woodworking reference books from the period are quite rare (some say this is due to the solemn oath sworn by apprentices to keep the "arts and mysteries" of the craft secret), there are a few available. The following books will get you started, but there is no substitute for examining period work in person. Do whatever it takes to make this happen, as often as possible.

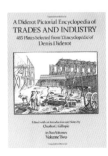

Diderot, D. & Gillispie, C. C., (1993). A Diderot Pictorial Encyclopedia of Trades and Industry: Manufacturing and the Technical Arts in Plates selected from ... of Denis Diderot. New York: Dover.

Moxon, J., & Schwarz, C. (2008). The art of joinery. Fort Mitchell, Ky.: Lost Art Press.

Nicholson, P., & Roberts, G. (2011). The mechanic's companion. Dedham. Mass.: Toolemera Press.

Roubo, A.J., Williams, D. C., Pietryka-Pagán, M., Lafargue, P., & R. (n.d.). To make as perfectly as possible: Roubo on marquetry.

Schwarz, C., & Moskowitz, J. (2009). The joiner and cabinet maker. Fort Mitchell, Ky.: Lost Art Press.

One other resource I greatly enjoy is the "Arts and Mysteries" column in *Popular Woodworking Magazine*. The June 2006 installment discussed the Charles Plumley Inventory, a listing of the tools owned and used by an early 18th-century Philadelphia cabinetmaker. This article will open your eyes to the excessive level of tooling in most modern shops.

Tools and shops

In recent decades, more ink has been spilled discussing tools, workbenches and shop organization than just about any other woodworking topic. However there are a such few books that have made my life as a period woodworker much easier.

Dunbar, M. (2014). Restoring, tuning & using classic woodworking tools. Cincinnati, Ohio: Popular Woodworking Books.

Elliott, T., & Pollak, E. (2003). A field guide to the makers of American wooden planes. Mendham, N.J.: Astragal Press.

Goodman, W. (1978). British planemakers from 1700 (2nd ed.). Needham Market: Arnold and Walker.

Pollak, E., & Pollak, M. (1987). A guide to American wooden planes and their makers (2nd ed.). Mendham, N.J.: Astragal Press.

Rees, J. (2012). The tool chest of Benjamin Seaton, 1797 (2nd ed.). Wakefield: Tool and Trades History Society.

Rosebrook, D., & Fisher, D. (2003). Wooden plow planes: A celebration of the planemakers' art. Mendham, N.J.: Astragal Press.

Schwarz, C. (2011). The anarchist's tool chest. Fort Mitchell, Ky.: Lost Art Press.

Shepherd, S. (2011). Shellac, linseed oil and paint. Salt Lake City, Utah: Full Chisel Press.

Shepherd, S. (2012). Shepherd's compleat early 19th century woodworker. Salt Lake City, Utah.: Full Chisel Press.

Sterre, G. (2001). Vier eeuwen Nederlandse schaven en schavenmakers = Four centuries of Dutch planes and planemakers. Leiden: Primavera Pers.

Underhill, R. (1981). The woodwright's shop: A practical guide to traditional woodcraft. Chapel Hill: University of North Carolina Press.

Underhill, R. (1983). The woodwright's companion: Exploring traditional woodcraft. Chapel Hill: University of North Carolina Press.

Underhill, R. (1986). The woodwright's workbook: Further explorations in traditional woodcraft. Chapel Hill: University of North Carolina Press.

Underhill, R. (1991). The woodwright's eclectic workshop. Chapel Hill: University of North Carolina Press.

Underhill, R. (1996). The woodwright's apprentice: Twenty favorite projects from the woodright's shop. Chapel Hill: University of North Carolina Press.

Underhill, R. (2008). The woodwright's guide: Working wood with wedge and edge. Chapel Hill: University of North Carolina Press.

Whelan, J. (1993). The wooden plane: Its history, form, and function. Mendham, N.J.: Astragal Press.

Whelan, J. (1996). Making traditional wooden planes. Mendham, N.J.: Astragal Press.

Techniques and joinery

"With Saw, Plane & Chisel" presents my idiosyncratic methods for reproducing historic joinery, based on the pieces I happen to have studied. These are far from the only reliable and period-correct joinery techniques.

The books listed below will give you information on a much wider variety of joints, and how to execute them in many different ways. When reading these books, be aware that many of the authors inject modern sensibilities into the work. So if you share my goal of period fidelity, don't let yourself get too carried away with the concept of objective perfection.

Ellis, G. (1987). Modern practical joinery: A treatise on the practice of joiner's work by hand and machine, for the use of workmen, architects, builders, and machinists. Fresno, Calif.: Linden Pub.

Frid, T. (2006). Tage Frid teaches woodworking: Three step-by-step guidebooks to essential woodworking techniques. Newtown, Conn.: Taunton Press.

Hasluck, P. N. (2007). The handyman's book: Tools, materials, and techniques for traditional woodworkers. Berkeley, Calif.: Skyhorse Pub.

Jones, B. E. (1998). The complete woodworker. Berkeley, Calif.: Ten Speed Press.

Kirby, I. J. (2001). The complete dovetail: Handmade furniture's signature joint. Fresno, Calif.: Linden Pub.

Talbot, A. (1980). Handbook of doormaking, windowmaking, and staircasing. New York: Sterling Pub.

Furniture styles and examples

One of my favorite things about learning to build period-correct furniture with hand tools is developing the ability to open a period furniture book, pick out a project, quickly work out the rough dimensions, and start working right away. Studying the work of the past will give you the confidence to start building without spending time looking for a measured drawing or worrying about finding exact dimensions. Basic case construction doesn't vary much. There are some regional differences, and changes in materials and joinery techniques across the centuries, but eventually you'll be able to just look at a piece and have a very good idea how it went together.

I am often asked where I get the ideas for the pieces I reproduce. I am most inspired by my visits to art museums, furniture collections, high-end antique stores and auction houses. Many museums have digitized their collections, creating incredibly valuable resources. The Metropolitan Museum of Art in New York City is the leader in this area. Auction catalogues and databases are another excellent resource. The books listed below will get you started and serve you well.

Chippendale, T. (1966). The gentleman & cabinetmaker's director. New York: Dover.

Downs, J. (1952). American furniture: Queen Anne and Chippendale periods. New York. The Macmillan Company.

Forman, B. M. (1987). American seating furniture, 1630-1730: An interpretive catalogue. New York: W.W. Norton.

Greene, J.P. (1996). American Furniture of the 18th century. Newtown: Taunton Press.

Heckscher, M. H. (1986). American furniture of the late colonial period: Selected essays and a catalogue of the collection of the Metropolitan Museum of Art. New York: Metropolitan Museum of Art.

Hornor, W. M. (1977). Hornor's blue book: Philadelphia furniture: William Penn to George Washington. Washington, D.C.: Highland House.

Jobe, B., Kaye, M., & Zea, P. (1984). New England furniture: The Colonial era: Selections from the Society for the Preservation of New England Antiquities. Boston: Houghton Mifflin.

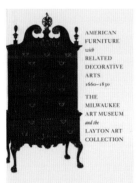

Jobe, B. W., Layton, F., & Ward, G. W. (1992). American furniture with related decorative arts, 1660 - 1830: The Milwaukee Art Museum and the Layton Art Collection. New York, NY: Hudson Hills Press.

Kettell, R. H. (1956). The pine furniture of early New England. New York: Dover Publications.

Kirk, J. T. (1984). American furniture and the British tradition to 1830. New York: Knopf.

Lindsey, J. L., Dunn, R. S., Carter, E. C., & Saunders, R. H. (1999). Worldly goods: The arts of early Pennsylvania, 1680-1758. Philadelphia, Pa.: Philadelphia Museum of Art.

Lockwood, L. V. (1926). Colonial furniture in America. New York: C. Scribner's Sons.

Margon, L. (1975). Construction of American furniture treasures: Measure drawings of selected museum pieces with complete information on their construction and reproduction... New York: Dover Publications.

Nutting, W. (1928). Furniture treasury. New York: Macmillan.

Sack, A. (2007). Fine points of furniture: Early American. Atglen, Pa.: Schiffer Publishing.

Safford, F. G. (2007). American furniture in the Metropolitan Museum of Art: Early Colonial period: The seventeenth century and William & Mary styles . New Haven, Conn.: Yale University Press.

Hardware

By Nancy Cogger

The finishing touch for any piece of furniture is the hardware. The decision of what hardware to choose should not be taken lightly, especially if your piece of furniture is an antique or is a reproduction of an antique. To truly enhance the furniture, authentic hardware appropriate to the time period of the piece of furniture is imperative. If original period hardware is not available, then a good quality reproduced copy will do nicely. When choosing reproduction hardware, a number of parameters must be considered. First and foremost to consider is the manufacturing method used in the reproduction of the hardware. Casting is the most common method used to make reproductions with lost wax casting process being the most common. Although not high tech and very labor intensive and by extension, more expensive than other brass manufacturing methods, lost wax casting produces the best quality copy. The wax is an excellent medium for capturing the minute details of the original, carrying them through to the copy. Sandcasting's ability to reproduce fine detail from a period original is dependent on the grain size of the sand. Sand with finer grains was used in colonial times, smaller than what is used today, so there is a loss of the crispness of the details in hardware reproduced by modern sandcasting.

Hardware can also be made by stamping and by extrusion. These methods are not used for one-off copies. They are better suited to a continuous production of a specific piece of hardware. Hardware made by stamping requires a die. This die, when pressure is applied onto the sheet of brass from the stamping machine, creates the pattern in the brass. Extruded hardware works well for items such as railings or trim. Hinges can be found made by extrusion. Both of these methods will produce hardware that is absolutely perfect, which is not what is desired when the intention you are seeking is one of period authenticity.

Once the method of casting is chosen, it is imperative that an original brass, which retains sharp details, is used to make the mold. A copy of a copy will yield a disappointing result. When reproducing period hardware, the composition of the alloy must be taken into account. The term *brass* defines a multitude of alloy variations. Brass is an alloy of copper and zinc. Other trace metals are often present, or are intentionally added to alter the brass for a specific purpose. For instance, lead is added to brass to aid in machining of brass.

If authenticity is your goal, then knowledge of the alloy used in the past is helpful. Hundreds of years ago and still today, yellow brass is the brass of choice for furniture hardware. An analysis of original brasses yielded the following percentages of copper, zinc and trace elements.

Each of the brasses analyzed also possessed some trace elements such as lead, chromium, nickel, tin, iron or silver. These elements were present in such small quantities that they would have a negligible effect on the look or mechanical properties of the brasses.

Manufacturers of brass furniture hardware today will also use yellow brass. The copper/zinc ratio of alloys that are classified as yellow brass has a large range. Here is a list of alloys which are described as Yellow Brass. The UNS number assigned to the alloy is the Unified Numbering System for Metals and Alloys.

ANALYSIS OF ORIGINAL BRASSES

ERA OF HARDWARE TESTED	COPPER	ZINC	TRACE
William & Mary	70.1%	26.2%	3.7%
Chippendale	74.3%	22.8%	2.9%
Queen Anne	74.6%	20.3%	5.1%
Sheraton	75.5%	22.9%	1.6%
Hepplewhite	77.7%	19.6%	2.7%

MODERN ALLOYS DESCRIBED AS YELLOW BRASS

UNS #	COPPER	ZINC	LEAD	TIN	ALUMINUM	IRON
C85200	72%	24%	3%	1%		
C85400	67%	29%	1%	3%		
C85500	61%	38.2%			0.8%	
C85700	63%	34.7%	1%	1%	0.3%	
C85800	58%	40%	1%	1%		
C86500	58%	39.5%	1%	0.5%	1%	1%

These modern alloys, like those in the past, have trace metals present. The trace metal present in the highest percentage, in both original yellow brass and in modern yellow brass is lead. In the original hardware tested, the lead percentages ranged from: not present – 2.5%. In modern yellow brass, the lead percentage range is: 0.4%–3/5%.

Lead is nearly insoluble in both copper and zinc, therefore it has little affect on the color of the hardware.

As the copper content lessens and it is replaced by less expensive zinc, the metal will become brittle. A higher copper-to-zinc ratio produces a softer brass with more malleability. This is quite important when fitting brasses onto a block front desk or chest. The brass must be able to bend over the shaped wood without cracking or bending unevenly.

Since there is zinc in the brass, any acids should be kept away from the brass fittings. Vinegar, which contains acetic acid, should never be used as a cleaner of brass as the acid will "eat away" at the zinc in the brass.

A completely reversible patination method, which quickly replicates the effect on hardware of the passage of time, is ammonia fumes. This method of patination knocks off the shine of brass and gives the hardware a

is defined as an alloy of copper and tin. However, in the vernacular of modern metallurgy, a bronze does not necessarily have to have any tin present. A silicon bronze, composed of only silicon and copper will be harder and will neither have the look nor the malleability of an antique brass or of modern yellow brass. Casters often prefer silicon bronze because it flows quite well in a mold and does not smoke. Manganese bronze is also used for furniture hardware for the ease with which it flows in casting. But the color of the hardware tends to have a silvery, brownish cast to it – not the golden color we expect from brass hardware. If you are seeking an authentic color in your hardware, yellow brass is the alloy to choose.

The next item which needs to be considered when purchasing reproduction hardware is the polishing method employed. Original hardware of course was hand-polished, which imbued it with a wonderful, warm color, leaving the concave areas a bit darker and the convex areas a bit brighter. Hand-polishing, which involves a person standing at a buffing wheel, polishing each piece of hardware, is still available. The hand-crafted, slightly imperfect look achieved with hand-polishing cannot be accomplished in any other way.

Another method used to polish brass hardware is by tumble or barrel polishing. Inside the tumbler are bits of very coarsely ground corn cob or walnut shell, which will polish the hardware in a very even manner. The end result is piece of hardware that tends to look a bit flat and too perfect. That bit of chiaroscuro which remains after hand polishing gives each piece of hardware added visual interest. If you are seeking to emulate period original hardware, then any method of brushing the brass or polishing in a way that produces a satin finish must be avoided.

If a period original is not available for copying, or if a brass manufacturer wants to create his/her own line of authentic looking hardware, one extremely important aspect of the hardware that I see which is often over looked is the thickness – or rather the thinness – of the period originals. Original William & Mary, Queen Anne and Chippendale hardware is less than $\frac{1}{16}$" thick. Very often, due to current automated manufacturing techniques, a plate less than $\frac{1}{16}$" thick is very expensive and difficult to produce. However, newly reproduced hardware, which can measure as much as $\frac{1}{8}$" thick, no longer possesses that "authentic look". When the bending of a plate is required, a plate $\frac{1}{8}$" thick will not be the ticket. A thinner plate, less than $\frac{1}{16}$" thick, can

lovely, warm, subdued appearance. If the patination process time is lengthened, the hardware will continue to darken to a very authentic looking dark brown.

However, ammonia is a stress corrosion cracking agent for brass, so this method must be used very judiciously. This was first observed by British soldiers in the 1800s in India. During the monsoon season, they stored their brass cartridges in horse barns. Many brass cartridges were found to be cracked, especially at the point where the case was crimped to the bullet. The ammonia from the horse urine, combined with the residual stress in the cold-drawn metal of the cartridges, was responsible for the cracking. Some of the other methods of patination that I have investigated can leave the hardware with a muddy, opaque look or the patination simply screams, "Faked!"

Instead of using yellow brass, some current hardware manufacturers prefer the silicon bronze alloy which has neither zinc nor tin. Historically bronze be bent to fit the curves of Bombay chests and block front furniture.

Another detail seen in antique hardware is the beveling of the edges of the plates. When the plates have beveled edges, they look right, and not as if they were cut out with a cookie cutter. If you are purchasing stamped hardware, check for beveling of the edges of the plates.

Speaking of cookie cutter perfection; when you have a piece replicated from a period original, there is an indefinable charm that comes from the signs of age, the slightly imperfect outline of the plate or the engraved patterns on the William & Mary plates which are not perfect mirror images from one side of the plate to the other. These little idiosyncrasies give the original hardware a certain charm that may be difficult to create when designing and making a new piece of hardware.

If a new piece of hardware if being designed, it is best to harken back to the details of the original hardware of that era if you are to produce an authentic looking piece of hardware. Study originals and don't stray too far from their patterns. Manufacturers who have not taken the time to study the details of period hardware often create some very odd, and in my opinion, very unattractive chimera. I have seen inventive combinations of hardware styles, such as a Chippendale plate in a bizarre, distorted shape which caused the bail to fall below the plate. The bail, which rested on the wood of the drawer, was held in place by turned head posts, normally only used with rosette pulls or on Hepplewhite hardware. The bail had a very odd kink instead of an elegant swan-neck shape. And to add insult to injury, the bail was turned, in the style of William & Mary. This aberrant piece of hardware, and others of the same ilk, will never complement a piece of fine furniture, be it an original or a reproduction. When designing a new piece of hardware, being true to the hardware styles of the past will hold you in good stead. By carefully considering all the factors involved in the production of brass furniture hardware, you should now be able to choose the hardware which will show your furniture to its best advantage.

Period Furniture Styles: A Historian's Perspective

By Robert F. Trent

Author's note: At the outset of each project chapter, I have provided a furniture-maker's perspective on the period and style at hand, using the popular terms for both. For an art historian's perspective on the periods and styles, I turned to Robert F. Trent, who generously contributed the following to this book. —Z.D.

Mannerist

Other names: Seventeenth-Century, Jacobean, Age of Oak, Pilgrim Century

Date ranges: In Italy, 1420-1600; in northern Europe, 1560-1630; in America, 1620-1690

Principal characteristics: Joined (frame and panel) construction, slightly eccentric classical ornament and wet wood joinery practice.

In Anglo-America, this style was practiced everywhere, but more survives from New England than from the Middle Colonies or the Old South. Americans rarely use the term "Mannerism" and have poor focus on what it means.

The generation of Michelangelo wanted to "exceed the Ancients," meaning the Romans, so they introduced complex variations in ornament. Through the medium of artists and thousands of design prints, the style spread to northern Europe and was further developed by strapwork ornament. England picked up the style mostly from France and the Netherlands.

The New England versions of this style were somewhat varied. The basic object was a joined or paneled chest with sunkwork ornament on the frame and panels. A second variant, derived from London practice and transmitted to Boston and New Haven, was an applied ornament style, wherein plaques, mouldings, half-columns and other architectural ornaments were glued to a joined structure. This applied ornament variant also tended to feature walnut and tropical hardwoods as the primary wood, in a distinctively Italianate way.

While New England furniture in the Mannerist style is well-known, other variants practiced by the Dutch in New York are less studied, save for the immense clothes cupboards called "kasten." Very little survives from Pennsylvania and the South.

Early Baroque

Other names: Louis XIV, William & Mary, Age of Walnut

Date range: In Italy and France, 1620-1690; in England, 1680-1710; in America, 1700-1730

Principal characteristics: high-backed chairs, first heavily upholstered easy chairs and settees; dovetailed board cases with applied thin veneers of figured woods; a great variety of tables for specific rituals.

The early baroque style in America was largely dependent on English versions of French courtly forms developed under Louis XIV. High-backed seating with naturalistic carved crests, arms and front stretchers were popular, as were chairs with cane seats and backs. Case pieces made a major shift from graviportal, horizontal designs to tall light structures perched on turned legs. The cases were made with dovetailed boards, which made them lighter in weight but also imposed structural problems. Tables proliferated into oval leaf tables for dining and other smaller forms for tea drinking, dressing and writing.

Boston, Newport, New York and Philadelphia developed regional variants of early Baroque forms, sometimes intermixed with stylistic and structural features of ethnic groups like the Dutch, the Germans and the French. Another important aspect of the style was Asian influence, particularly black-and-gold decoration based on Asian lacquer.

Late Baroque

Other names: Regence, Louis XV, Queen Anne, George I, Age of Walnut

Date range: In England and the Netherlands, 1715-1750; in America, 1725-1760

Principal characteristics: Lower backs on chairs in emulation of Asian and Louis XV chairs; some seating has "compass" or horseshoe-shaped seat plans; continued use of dovetailed board cases, but with an increasing reliance on figured walnut and mahogany rather than veneers; overall the introduction of the sawn and shaved cabriole leg on almost all furniture save for chests-on-chests or clock cases.

Sustained Asian influence led to Chinese-looking seating and the widespread use of japanning, or simulated lacquer. Asian influence also is seen in furniture hardware. At the same time, the fluid lines of Regence and early Louis XV furniture also impacts carving on all forms. Many more artisans arrive in many American ports, resulting in tension between entrenched woodworking families and newcomers. As yet there is relatively little transmission of designs via graphic sources. Boston remains a major stylistic center for the English-speaking colonies, but other centers like New York and Philadelphia are swiftly reaching maturity. Unlike other cities, Philadelphia has large populations of German and Irish artisans who establish important features of the city style.

New structural practices emerge for the high chest of drawers and the dressing table, both of which now have cabriole legs with squared upper sections that receive tenons from the sides. Less innovation was required to integrate cabriole legs in tables and seating. Several regional schools employed framing with flat rails into which the tops of the legs were dovetailed or plugged. That variant of construction was common in upholstery frames.

Strong ethnic enclaves in certain colonies practiced European styles and furniture forms, notably the kast in Dutch areas, the schrank in German areas, and painted chests in many centers with French Dutch and German settlers.

Rococo

Other names: Louis XV, Chippendale, Age of Mahogany

Date range: In England, 1735-1775; in America, 1750-1790

Principal characteristics: Retention of most furniture forms, but all are now overlaid with Rococo carving that displays shells, scrolling acanthus foliage with whiplash tips, and occasional figurative carving of birds, Aesop's Fables and other pictorial sources. Scroll pediments become more common. Carved claw-and-ball feet become ubiquitous. Many table forms receive substantial amounts of carving on tops, shafts, knees, skirts and feet.

The Rococo was one of the most complex periods to date. Increased wealth levels led to larger-scale production in many urban centers, and ports or administrative centers in the South also developed major cabinetmaking shops, notably at Williamsburg and Charleston. Development of large populations in piedmont areas increased production of vernacular furniture, often with strong European structural and stylistic traits.

Driving much of this was immigration of skilled artisans from England and Europe, as well as the circulation of books and loose sheets of ornamental prints. For the first time, American cabinetmakers were making furniture based on published designs, rather than shop traditions. This is not to say that some centers didn't develop regional types. Notable examples are the bombé and block-front case pieces of Mass., the block-and-shell case pieces of R.I., the scroll-pedimented high chests of drawers of Philadelphia, and the immense bookcases and linen presses of Charleston.

Rococo carving required rigorous drawing and hand skills. In those centers where such carving was in demand for architectural and furniture, the immigration of London carvers raised the level of quality considerably. However, most furniture had little carving – mostly claw-and-ball feet, simplified leafage on the knees, and a bit of carving on drawers or chair crests.

Seating changed quite dramatically as the rounded forms of the late Baroque yielded to the straighter forms of the Rococo, especially the crest rails of chairs, which assumed the form of a cupid's bow, and the banisters in the backs of chairs, which began to be pierced in scroll or Gothic patterns.

Neoclassical
Other names: Federal, Adam

Date range: In England, 1765-1795; in America, 1709-1815

Principal characteristics: Light, even delicate forms inspired by revivals of Greek and Roman architecture, frescos and ceramics. While Herculaneum and Pompeii are the most frequently cited sources, the earliest neoclassical objects in Europe relied on Mannerist and Baroque monuments. After all, Mannerism was based in part on Roman frescos excavated about 1490-1510. However, as Europeans traveled to the eastern Mediterranean and began measuring Greek architectural monuments, Greek forms became more current. Major publications about Greek pottery were also consulted. An important impulse was a reliance on strong geometric forms and a rejection of Rococo leafage.

Neoclassical furniture began to impact American furniture in the late 1780s, but was not widely introduced until the mid-1790s. Certainly furniture designs published in London were one impulse, but French Louis XVI and Directoire furniture had an enormous impact, due in part to furniture brought to American from France by ambassadors, ministers and diplomats.

Seating transitioned completely to square- or urn-backed chairs seen in design books by Hepplewhite and Sheraton. These same sources prompted the transition from cabriole legs to turned or tapered forms. Most such designs required carved, painted or veneered decoration, thereby increasing costs. Tables went through a similar transition.

New case pieces included sideboards, cylinder or tambour desks, chests of drawers with elliptical or swept fronts, and new shapes for card tables. Many of these forms displayed veneering and complex stringing. Some gilding was introduced, but not as much as in the ensuing Late Neoclassical or Empire period.

INDEX

ABOUT THE AUTHOR

Zach Dillinger specializes in building early 18th century American furniture all with hand tools and period appropriate techniques. He is an active member of the Great Lakes Chapter of the Society of American Period Furniture Makers, and the Midwest Tool Collectors Association. He has written for *Popular Woodworking Magazine*, *Fine Woodworking*, *American Period Furniture*, *Mortise & Tenon Magazine*, *Early American Life Magazine* and numerous websites including his own, *The Eaton County Woodworker*. His work has been adjudged to be Museum Quality by *Early American Life* and has been juried into that publication's prestigious "Directory of Traditional American Crafts" for the past three years. When not making furniture, he enjoys playing tennis and working on his 1926 Ford Model T. Zach lives in Michigan with his wife April, their daughter Abigail and a gaggle of pets and livestock.

With Saw, Plane & Chisel. Copyright © 2016 by Zachary Dillinger. Printed and bound in China. All rights reserved. No part of this book may be reproduced in any form or by any electronic or mechanical means including information storage and retrieval systems without permission in writing from the publisher, except by a reviewer, who may quote brief passages in a review. Published by Popular Woodworking Books, an imprint of F+W Media, Inc., 10151 Carver Rd. Blue Ash, Ohio, 45242. First edition.

Distributed in Canada by Fraser Direct
100 Armstrong Avenue
Georgetown, Ontario L7G 5S4
Canada

Distributed in the U.K. and Europe by
F+W Media International, LTD
Brunel House, Ford Close
Newton Abbot
Devon TQ12 4PU, UK
Tel: (+44) 1626 323200
Fax: (+44) 1626 323319

Visit our website at popularwoodworking.com or our consumer website at shopwoodworking.com for more woodworking information.

Other fine Popular Woodworking Books are available from your local bookstore or direct from the publisher.

ISBN-13: 978-1-4403-4339-1

20 19 18 17 16   5 4 3 2 1

Editor: *Asa Christiana*
Designers: *Daniel T. Pessell & Angela Wilcox*
Production Coordinator: *Debbie Thomas*

a content + ecommerce company

Read This Important Safety Notice

To prevent accidents, keep safety in mind while you work. Use the safety guards installed on power equipment. When working on power equipment, keep fingers away from saw blades, wear safety goggles to prevent injuries from flying wood chips and sawdust, wear hearing protection and consider installing a dust vacuum to reduce the amount of airborne sawdust in your woodshop. Don't wear loose clothing or jewelry when working on power equipment. Tie back long hair to prevent it from getting caught in your equipment. People who are sensitive to certain chemicals should check the chemical content of any product before using it. The authors and editors who compiled this book have tried to make the contents as accurate and correct as possible. Plans, illustrations, photographs and text have been carefully checked. All instructions, plans and projects should be carefully read, studied and understood before beginning construction. Due to the variability of local conditions, construction materials, skill levels, etc., neither the author nor Popular Woodworking Books assumes any responsibility for any accidents, injuries, damages or other losses incurred resulting from the material presented in this book. Prices listed for supplies and equipment were current at the time of publication and are subject to change.

Metric Conversion Chart

Inches	Centimeters	2.54
Centimeters	Inches	0.4
Feet	Centimeters	30.5
Centimeters	Feet	0.03
Yards	Meters	0.9
Meters	Yards	1.1

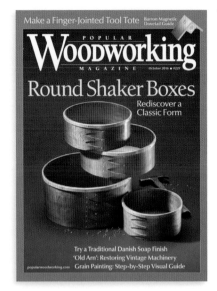
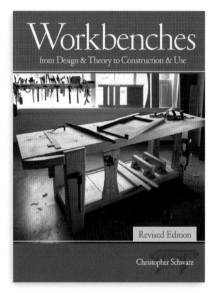
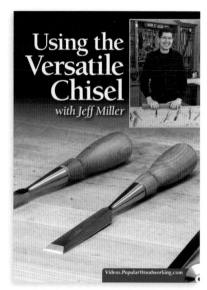
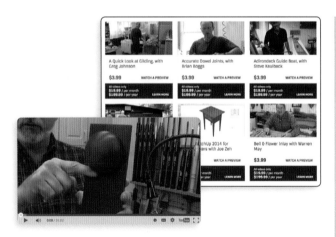